Twayne's English Authors Series

Sylvia E. Bowman, *Editor*

INDIANA UNIVERSITY

Benjamin Disraeli

TEAS 68

Benjamin Disraeli

By RICHARD A. LEVINE

University of California, Riverside

Twayne Publishers, Inc.   ::   New York

PR
4087
.L4

66680

For Felice

Preface

A curiosity of our age of criticism is that Benjamin Disraeli the novelist has not received more attention. Of our major critics only F. R. Leavis has expressed surprise that Disraeli has not been "rediscovered." In *The Great Tradition* he observes that "the novelist who has not been revived is Disraeli. Yet, though he is not one of the great novelists, he is so alive and intelligent as to deserve permanent currency, at any rate in the trilogy *Coningsby, Sybil,* and *Tancred;* his own interests as expressed in these books—the interests of a supremely intelligent politician who has a sociologist's understanding of civilization and its movement in his time—are so mature."[1] Leavis is correct on two counts: Disraeli does deserve a fresh examination, and it is indeed the Young England trilogy which emerges as his most interesting work. The purpose of this study is, therefore, to examine Disraeli's novels with particular focus on *Coningsby, Sybil,* and *Tancred.* Not only are these three works Disraeli's major novels, but there has been no extended discussion of them in recent years.

In the last thirty-five years, scarcely one hundred items have been published dealing with Disraeli's literary works, and of these perhaps one half are mere notes. More interesting is the fact that interpretive readings of the novels have been infrequent and, by and large, have addressed themselves to the novels as autobiography and as social history. Certainly a closer look at Disraeli's novels is needed. The reader interested in the English novel, in the nineteenth century or in English politics and history should know *Coningsby, Sybil,* and *Tancred.* There is obviously less cogency for such a reader's familiarity with Disraeli's eight other novels, but they are important in furthering our understanding of the author and his times. Not, of course, that an avid reader should pull these Disraeli novels from the shelf sooner than those by Charles Dickens or George Eliot. But Disraeli was a significant and intensely interesting man and, at times, a fascinating writer. He was not only a Prime Minister, an acute politician, and a brilliant statesman, but he was also a keen observer of the motivations which shaped men and their institutions. And his novels yield many of Disraeli's most penetrating conceptions of life and history as well as politics.

This study is an introduction to those novels (rather than to Disraeli's total literary production). Indeed, the purpose of the series in which this volume appears is to offer the reader a critical but introductory overview of the author's works. In the present case, this intent is coupled with a particular point of view regarding Disraeli's novels. We shall see developed in the major novels much that is said with less artistic effect in the minor works. Even when not wholly in control of either subject matter or technique, Disraeli's mind dwelt on certain intellectual, emotional, and ideological problems. My discussion of the early and late novels deals with (1) their ideas and themes in relation to their author's most significant works, (2) their place in the development of Disraeli's control of the novel form, and (3) their relationship to both autobiography and history.

The key to my interpretation of the Young England novels is Disraeli's view of the past which forms the sub-structure for his readings of society, religion, and history. By no means do I suggest, however, that Disraeli was either a systematic or deep thinker in these areas; but his novels are permeated with the evidences of his concerned, sporadic inquiries into the relevance of the past. The feudal past with its hierarchical ordering of society is a cardinal factor in Disraeli's thought. The *noblesse oblige* of the aristocracy, Carlyle's view of the Kantian distinction between the worlds of phenomena and noumena, and the theory of the hero are all cogent concerns in Disraeli's conception of social organization. In religion, Disraeli's rendering of the Hebraeo-Christian Church and a renewed belief in the fundamental spiritual nature of man are the dominant characteristics. For many of Disraeli's characters (as for many flesh-and-blood Victorians) the relevance of the Primitive Church became great as their age sought authority in the midst of growing skepticism.

[8]

Disraeli saw the historical process as spiraling and organic; for, just as there is an Apostolic succession in religion, so was there a vital continuity in history.

Indeed, as we shall see, the years preceding the Young England novels witnessed a rebirth of interest in historical studies and in the formulation of a new philosophy of history. Especially in the Young England trilogy do we encounter these motifs as Disraeli presents his most successful novels in depth of intellectual and ideological complexity. And always the reader must be aware of the tension between the "facts" imaginatively developed in the novels and the real facts of Disraeli's life of social and political involvement.

Thus the approach of this discussion is twofold: a broad and admittedly "ideas" reading of the Young England trilogy and a critical as well as thematic survey of the other novels, especially as they relate to both Disraeli's later ideas and to the trilogy. Although my emphasis is on Disraeli's fiction, I cannot ignore the age out of which the novels grew. When dealing with almost any Victorian novelist, and especially with one who was also a practicing politician, the reader must consider political and social questions which arise from the entire "condition of England" problem. So it is that before beginning a discussion of the novels, this study presents a series of "introductory notes" which will offer the reader (especially the reader not very familiar with the subject) a glimpse of the biographical and historical backgrounds of Disraeli and his fiction. Many of these notes will be developed in greater detail in subsequent pages of the book.

I should like to call the reader's attention to Robert Blake's *Disraeli* which I mention in the bibliography but do not incorporate into the text of this study. Due to the complexities of bringing out a book in an undertaking as large as Twayne's English Authors Series, this book—although completed before the publication of Blake's—follows Blake into print. I mention this fact for two reasons: First, I wish to acknowledge my deep respect for that brilliant biography of our common subject; secondly, I am pleased to note that Blake and I are not far apart in our readings of the Young England novels.

A number of people have aided me in this study, and to them all I am grateful. In particular, I should like to thank Professors

Robert F. Gleckner and Robert L. Peters of the University of California, Riverside; Donald R. Howard of Johns Hopkins University; Donald A. Smalley of the University of Illinois; and William A. Madden of Indiana University.

My thanks also to the editors of *Nineteenth Century Fiction* for permission to reprint a portion of this book's Chapter 5 which appeared in the June, 1967, *NCF*.

Once I had thought that a writer's thanks to his wife was a mere convention of "prefacemanship." I have since learned the error of that view.

University of California
Riverside, California

Contents

Contents

Chronology

With the exception of a few important political statements and tracts, only the novels of Benjamin Disraeli's published work are listed completely. I include some of Disraeli's votes in Parliament to underscore the often close relationship between the ideas of the politician and those of the novelist.

1804   Benjamin Disraeli born on Friday, December 21, to Isaac and Maria D'Israeli.

1817   Baptized into the Church of England, July 31.

1821   Begins three years with a firm of solicitors in London; speculates in stock market.

1825   Makes abortive attempts at launching a journalistic career with *The Representative*; loses money in mining venture and heavily in debt.

1826   Publication of *Vivian Grey*; friendship with the Austens, who were instrumental in aiding Disraeli's literary career.

1827   Publication of the sequel to *Vivian Grey*.

1831   Publication of *The Young Duke*; Disraeli visits Jerusalem.

1832   He meets Mrs. Wyndham Lewis; publication of *Contarini Fleming*; twice in this year Disraeli is defeated as an Independent parliamentary candidate from Wycombe.

1833   Publication of *Alroy*.

1835   Disraeli defeated again at Wycombe; he joins the Conservative Party; at Taunton, Disraeli suffers another defeat, this time as a Tory; publication of *The Vindication of the English Constitution*.

1836   Publication of the "Letters of 'Runnymede'" and *The Spirit of Whiggism*.

1837   Publication of *Henrietta Temple* and *Venetia*; Disraeli elected with Wyndham Lewis as MP from Maidstone;

gives maiden speech in Parliament (December 7); votes
for the repeal of the Poor Law.

1838 Wyndham Lewis dies; Disraeli attends Queen Victoria's
coronation.

1839 Disraeli gives great speech on Chartism; marries Mrs.
Wyndham Lewis.

1843 He leads the "Young England party" in Parliament.

1844 Publication of *Coningsby*; opposes new Poor Law and
supports Factory Reform Laws; delivers the "Young England Manifesto" at Manchester Athenaeum to an enormous
audience. ("It was the culminating point in the glory of
Young England"—Monypenny.)

1845 Publication of *Sybil*.

1846 Disraeli attacks the Corn Law; attacks Peel and supports
the Whigs.

1847 Publication of *Tancred*; his mother dies; speaks on Jewish
disabilities laws, insisting (as he does in *Tancred*) that
there is an intimate and binding relationship between
Judaism and Christianity.

1848 His father dies.

1851 *Lord George Bentinck: A Political Biography.*

1852 Chancellor of the Exchequer; Ministry defeated.

1853 Receives an honorary degree from Oxford.

1858 Chancellor of the Exchequer once again.

1859 Ministry defeated.

1866 Again Chancellor of the Exchequer.

1868 Becomes Prime Minister; his Ministry defeated; Mrs. Disraeli made a peeress, Viscountess Beaconsfield.

1870 Publication of *Lothair*; collected edition of his works, with
General Preface, begins to appear in November.

1872 Lady Beaconsfield dies.

1874 Prime Minister (1874-1880); offers a baronetcy to Tenny-
son and the Grand Cross of the Order of the Bath to Carlyle. Both refuse.

1875 Majority of shares in the Suez Canal Company purchased.

1876 Gives last speech in the House of Commons; accepts peerage and is the first Earl of Beaconsfield.

1880 Conservatives are defeated and Disraeli gives up the
Prime Ministership; publication of *Endymion*.

1881 Dies on Tuesday, April 19.

CHAPTER 1

Introductory Notes

I *A Curious Baptism*

ON the morning of July 21, 1817, Sharon Turner, the distinguished historian, turned down the front walk and into the large house at No. 6 Bloomsbury Square, London. He was in the house only a brief time before the door opened again and two men and a boy emerged: Turner, Isaac D'Israeli, and his thirteen-year-old son, Benjamin. They proceeded directly to St. Andrew's Church, Holborn, where in a brief ceremony the boy was baptized into the Church of England by the Reverend J. Thimbleby. Turner was the godfather and delighted in the service which he had done so much to bring about, but the elder D'Israeli seemed unmoved throughout the proceedings. Much later in life, Lord Beaconsfield pointed out that "It was Mr. Sharon Turner who persuaded my father—after much trouble—to allow his children to be baptized. He, one day, half consented, upon which Mr. Turner called on the day following and took us off to St. Andrew's, Holborn."[1]

So it was that at the symbolic age of thirteen, instead of entering into brotherhood with those who shared his own religious heritage, Benjamin Disraeli was accepted as a member of the Anglican Church. The situation was curious. Isaac D'Israeli did not really care about religion. He was certainly no longer a practicing Jew, but he was by no means a Christian. Benjamin's mother, Maria, was distressed at the social handicap of her religion and therefore was pleased at the conversion; Turner felt it imperative if the D'Israeli children were to make their way in the world of Anglican England. He had frequently urged Isaac to approve the move, claiming that the blank page between the Old Testament and the New Testament might be a comfortable resting place for the parent, but it would never do for the children. Isaac's rather careless attitude can be seen by the fact that his four children were baptized on three different days: Ralph and James on July 11, Benjamin on July 21, and Sarah on August 28, 1817.

Although the father was unaware of it at the time, the day of Benjamin's baptism was a significant one. For it was with this entrance of a Jew into the Church of England that the future opened for the novelist and particularly for the Prime Minister. And more important in the years to come, Disraeli the alien and outsider was born on July 21, 1817. His desire for respect and his ambition for success and power were heightened by the possibilities gained through his conversion. However, as we shall see later, the background which he nominally left at the age of thirteen remained with him and shaped much of his later thought.

II *England in an Age of Flux*

England in the nineteenth century produced an exceptionally large number of fascinatingly complex personalities. It was not at all uncommon for Victorian Englishmen to work simultaneously in several fields. There were clergymen who were also creative writers; both Charles Kingsley and John Henry Newman, for example, wrote novels. John Ruskin, scholar, critic, and essayist, founded a corporate social movement, the St. George Guild. William Ewart Gladstone wrote religious tracts and Homer criticism. Ebenezer Elliott, a middle-class iron manufacturer, composed and published poetry. And so the list goes. The Victorian Age witnessed a keen interest on the part of many of its members in various and often apparently uncongenial areas of life. Perhaps not since the Renaissance had England produced so many versatile and far-ranging men—men whose breadth of interests moved far beyond their peculiarly personal concerns and activities.

One of the major factors which helped shape such a situation was the "condition of England" question and its many ramifications. The nineteenth century in England was, for the most part, not a calm age; it was an age of anxiety, an age of flux. Traditional institutions—religious, social, and political—were challenged from every corner. Individual man's relationships to his church, class, and government were coming under a new scrutiny. Man was no longer sure of these relationships; he had to examine their very basis or, at least, have them examined for him. Wesleyanism, the Oxford Movement, parliamentary Reform Bills, Chartism, Utilitarianism, a new Traditionalism, the impact of science, and, above all, the Industrial Revolution made new intellectual and emotional demands upon the Victorian man.[2] The traditional relationships between men and their fellow men, and between men and their institutions were crumbling.

Often the newly created or suggested relationships were unsatisfactory. For example, in theory, the Industrial Revolution was a magnificent success, a giant step into the future, supplying the mechanized means for achieving undreamed-of progress. In practice, however, this same Industrial Revolution led to social problems of such magnitude that many thoughtful Englishmen could not help viewing it as, at best, a dubious blessing. Never before in modern times had an age been forced so thoroughly to re-evaluate the very roots of its existence. Never before had a people been faced with so many disruptive shocks—shocks brought on by the upheaval of values which their grandparents in the eighteenth century had considered permanent and true. In fact, by the mid-nineteenth century, the average Victorians (those, at least, above the great class of paupers in the new industrial centers) found it best to ignore such questions and to settle down to enjoy complacently their greater salary, the nation's "peace," and the "great exhibitions." But others refused to be engulfed by mid-century complacency as they saw great problems and responded to them.

The complex social, moral, and political problems of Victorian England produced the unusually large number of many-sided intellects. In an age shaken by the onslaughts of science and technology, poverty and squalor, Rome and enthusiasm, Utilitarianism and radicalism, thinking men had to take sides—or, at least, they had to consider the issues carefully. And to consider the issues, they had to become aware of them—a difficult task in any age, but a greater one for men in an age of such great change. Such, then,—in broad terms—was the *milieu* out of which came the novelist and statesman Benjamin Disraeli.

III *A Family of Letters*

Disraeli was born into a family perfectly suited to produce a man of letters. His father, Isaac, instead of following the parental plans so carefully laid for him, had turned to the world of the arts rather than to one of business. Isaac was an enigma to his parents, and neither his father nor his mother could understand this dreamy-eyed, "impractical" young man whose aversion to business was as great as his love for poetry. Benjamin writes of his father's fondness for poetry and of his attempts to forward this interest in an alien environment:

The crisis arrived when, after months of abstraction and irritability, my father produced a poem. For the first time my grandfather was seriously alarmed. The loss of one of his argosies, uninsured, could not have filled him with more blank dismay. His idea of a poet was formed from one of the prints of Hogarth hanging in his room, where an unfortunate wight in a garret was inditing an ode to riches, while dunned for his milk-score.[3]

His parents could force him into the counting houses of England, France, and Holland, but they could never force his spirit to accept such work. Finally, when the elder Benjamin D'Israeli (Isaac's father) retired from business to live out the remainder of his life enjoying the fortune he had amassed, the son was free.

Once assured of financial independence, Isaac immediately quit business and entered the literary world of London. While still in his twenties, he published his *Curiosities of Literature,* which established him as a man of letters. J. A. Froude points out a fact cardinally important in the future of the Prime Minister's father:

Isaac D'Israeli, having the advantage of a good fortune, escaped the embarrassments which attend a struggling literary career. His circumstances were easy. He became intimate with distinguished men; and his experiences in Paris [where he had remained until the eve of the Revolution] had widened and liberalised his mind.[4]

Isaac could cultivate the world of letters on his own terms and at his leisure. Books and writers became his world. To be sure, he continued to write poetry and literary commentary; but, in the main, he remained an enthusiastic consumer of literature and a devoted friend of writers.

Isaac threw himself into his literary pursuits.

His pen was never idle, but it was to note and to register, not to compose. His researches were prosecuted every morning among the MSS. of the British Museum, while his own ample collections permitted him to pursue his investigations in his own library into the night.[5]

All of English literature became Isaac's domain. Among his several published works, the *Amenities of Literature* (1843), published late in his life, best indicates the great breadth of his reading. In all, there are seventy essays dealing with writers from Chaucer to Shakespeare to the Romantics, whom he loved best of all, and to Byron who, for D'Israeli, was the pre-eminent Romantic poet. D'Israeli also loved history and historical inquiry: "The amount of emphasis Disraeli places on a miscellany like Arnolde's Chronicle [in the *Amenities*] is a bit out of line. . . . In fact, Disraeli's preoccupation with the historical point of view is manifest."[6] George K. Anderson suggests that D'Israeli followed the example of Henry Hallam "because of his personal liking for history and the kind of historical writing which Hallam so brilliantly exemplified."[7] This interest in historical writing is significant, for we later see the same predisposition in Benjamin. Indeed, the younger Disraeli announced that his three favorite areas of reading were history, theology, and classics.[8]

In his personal life, Isaac D'Israeli became a solid, middle-class English subject. He married a Jewish Englishwoman, Maria Basevi, and reared a family of three boys and a girl (a fifth child, Naphthali, died in infancy). On December 21, 1804, the second child and the favorite son, Benjamin, was born. According to the records of London's Bevis Marks synagogue, Benjamin was received into the Jewish religion. Realizing the difficulties that a young Jewish boy would encounter in English public schools, Isaac entered his son in a small private academy, Mr. Potticany's at Blackheath. The young Disraeli learned little there and apparently little more at a subsequent school, Hingham Hall, but he was a brilliant boy and had his father's extensive library at his disposal.

In this magnificent private library (which contained 25,000 volumes at Isaac's death) Disraeli gained his early education. From his father's books and literary friends, and encouraged by his father's sympathetic attitude toward his literary interests, Benjamin entered the world of literature and ideas. "Young Disraeli's formal schooling ended, at his own insistence, when he was sixteen and when he was drawn to Isaac's library. Here . . . he read voraciously in an effort to learn his own identity. School had told him nothing about himself. He had found the mouths of teachers full of only 'words,' but great books, he discovered, delighted him because they were written by great men who had feelings akin to his own."[9] B. R. Jerman tells us that it was at this time in Benjamin's development that Isaac introduced his son "into his [Isaac's] own small circle of friends, where the greats and the near-greats of literature exchanged anecdotes, many of which Ben transferred to paper and later utilized in his novels. For a time, then, Disraeli occupied himself with the wonderful world of learning"; and he longed to write.[10]

IV Isaac's "Non-Jewishness"

In 1817 three events took place which were to be of immense importance in Benjamin Disraeli's life: his grandfather died, his father succeeded to the family fortune, and the Disraeli family formally withdrew from the Jewish congregation. The first two events need little elucidation; but the third event is more complex. There has been much speculation as to the precise nature of both Isaac's and Benjamin's non-Jewishness. Only three facts emerge: (1) Isaac removed himself from his synagogue in 1817; (2) in the same year, his four children were, as we have seen, baptized into the Church of England; and (3) Isaac, himself, never formally entered the Christian fold.

In 1813 the elders of D'Israeli's Spanish and Portuguese Synagogue Saar Asamaim ("The Gate of Heaven") selected Isaac D'Israeli to become their Parnas or Presiding Warden. Isaac politely refused the office, and thus began what was to become a bitter correspondence between him and the Mahamad (the synagogue's presiding body). Isaac was told that, by having refused the position, he had become liable to a fine of forty pounds. He refused to pay, and the correspondence continued. Perhaps not wishing to hurt his father (a semi-active member of the congregation[11]), Isaac waited until after his father's death before he ended all correspondence completely with a letter in which he concluded: "I have patiently sought for protection against the absurd choice of two or three injudicious individuals, but I find that you as a body sanction what your own laws will not allow. I am not a fit member of your society, and I certainly am an aggrieved one. I must now close all future correspondence, and I am under the painful necessity of insisting that my name be erased from the list of your members. . . ."[12] So Isaac D'Israeli left his synagogue. He entered none of the other London synagogues, and, it appears, he preferred to remain without a particular religious commitment.

Friends now began to urge Isaac to allow his children to have a religious affiliation even if he himself desired none. They, like Sharon Turner, pointed out that it was cruel to leave his children "in the disabilities of a religion from the practice of which they had been withdrawn."[13] The promptings and advice of his friends undoubtedly formed the primary reason for Isaac's having his children baptized. He remained without religion, although his final resting place is in the parish church at Bradenham in Buckinghamshire. If this, then, was the father's relationship with his religion, what was the son's?

Did Benjamin leave Judaism reluctantly? Or did he embrace Christianity immediately? D. L. Murray correctly implies that this point is, at best, conjectural. Since Disraeli never clearly discussed this event of his youth, Murray's comment concerning the baptismal rites is probably as much as we can say about the young Disraeli's response to the ceremony: "We cannot tell with what thoughts he [Benjamin] approached the rite, or what fancies may have kindled his vivid, dark eyes. Did he know any fleeting sense of sacrifice? Did his mind stray a moment to the venerable synagogue. . . ?"[14] Most critics share Murray's conclusion; there is no way of knowing how Benjamin reacted to joining the Christian religion. However, one critic, the distinguished Anglo-Jewish scholar, Cecil Roth, offers an interesting conjecture on this subject.

. . . the parish registers make it quite clear that while the two surviving younger boys, Ralph and James, were baptized by the Reverend William Hart Coleridge (the poet's nephew) on July 11th, 1817, Benjamin was not with them; his turn came ten days later, on July 21st, the ceremony being performed by the Reverend (subsequently Professor) J. Thimbleby, their sister Sarah following only on August 28th.

This is the first of a series of mysteries, or at least coincidences, associated with the religious life of the later Prime Minister. Why the baptism should have taken place in instalments, the younger children coming first and having the ceremony performed by someone who stood in obvious literary connection with their father, is extremely difficult to understand. (Had the delay been due to Ben's illness, he would certainly have mentioned the fact.) But one may hazard the conjecture, put forward indeed with the utmost hesitancy, that the young Benjamin's religious education and Hebraic consciousness (which was afterwards so noteworthy) were by this time so pronounced that he may have raised objections to what his father flaccidly proposed, and that when Mr. Sharon Turner called on the morning of July 11th only the two younger boys [eight and four in 1817] were willing to accompany him. Their elder sister, Sarah [fifteen at this time], always very close to Benjamin, might have shared in the revolt, and stood out a little longer; or possibly it may not have been considered that the formalities mattered so much in the case of a girl.[15]

The conjecture aside, Roth focuses attention on Disraeli's Hebraic consciousness which played an important role in the life of Disraeli the novelist.

From the age of thirteen, then, Disraeli was a member of the Anglican Church. Yet throughout his life, as several of his novels attest, Disraeli remained at heart a Hebrew. At the core of his religious philosophy was the cardinal fact that Christianity was completed Judaism. By the same token "those who profess to be Jews only he considers unfortunate in believing only the first part of their religion. . . ."[16] This commingling of Judaism and Christianity into what Disraeli labels the Hebraeo-Christian Church forms a significant theme in his trilogy, a theme which we shall later examine.

At this point in our discussion, then, we have seen the two most important strokes of fortune in the young Disraeli's life. First, he was born into a family predisposed to honor and encourage his literary inclinations. There is no question that Isaac saw much of himself mirrored in Benjamin and approved, well remembering another Benjamin's relationship with an intellectually gifted, literary-minded child. Second, Isaac D'Israeli helped clear the way to political fortune when he had his children enter the Church of England.

V *His Literary Career*

Disraeli's literary career was as prolific as it was diverse. In addition to his novels, Disraeli wrote a biography, a play, poems, short stories, essays, and, of course, political commentary. When he was twenty-two, his first novel, *Vivian Grey* (1828), was published. It caused a sensation, but only because it contained an abundance of flimsily disguised portraits of real members of fashionable society. This factitious interest, coupled with the fact that the author was anonymous, attracted readers to the book. It was Bulwer Lytton who had brought Disraeli into fashionable society, and Disraeli's early works were influenced by Lytton. Fortunately, Disraeli entered Parliament in 1837, and his career as a "silver fork" novelist came to an end. (The years of the ambitious, dandified young novelist are well covered in other places.[17]) From his parliamentary days on, Disraeli's literary productions were to be, in the main, serious, often heavily didactic works incorporating his deepest views of society, politics, history, and religion.

Like Disraeli's own works, the novel generally had undergone a change in its position from the 1830's to the 1840's. In the 1830's the novel had come upon the bleakest days it would face in the century, for the public appetite could be satisfied only by news of public events and politics. In the *Athenaeum* for May 12, 1832, we read that "No one talks of literature in these stormy and changeful times . . . no attention is paid to anything but speculations on reform and change of rules."[18] Kathleen Tillotson, commenting on this situation, says that "Fiction had to be disguised as *Illustrations of Political Economy* to succeed."[19] But, she adds, in the 1840's "people read novels more than ever; for the novel was now ready and able to absorb and minister to their 'speculations on reform.' No longer does it belong to the world of indolent languid men on sofas, of Aesthetic Tea; to the 'sect' whose temple was Almack's and whose sacred books were fashionable novels. It belongs to the no-man's land on the frontier between the two nations. . . ."[20]

In this atmosphere Disraeli's trilogy was produced. The novel offered Disraeli the perfect vehicle. In his Preface to the fifth edition of *Coningsby* in 1849, Disraeli says: "It was not originally the intention of the writer to adopt the form of fiction as the instrument to scatter his suggestions, but after reflection he resolved to avail himself of a method which, in the temper of the times, offered the best chance of influencing opinion."[21]

VI *"Young England Movement"*

Disraeli had been in Parliament for only four years when, in 1841, a group of eager, brilliant young MP's gathered around him; he became their "master." This small group of men "had been educated together at Eton and Cambridge, and . . . were united not only by the memory of their school and college friendship, but by a common stock of ideas on questions of Church and state."[22] As we shall see, these young men, who came to be known as the "Young England Movement," were romantic in temperament, royalist in principle, and medieval and Catholic in sentiment. With Disraeli as their leader, they attempted to infuse into what they considered a decaying Tory party an awareness of its true principles. Appalled by the lack of great guiding principles in English life, they lamented the state of the people; they distrusted Utilitarianism, democracy, and the middle class; and—most important for this study—they urged Disraeli to put in print the aims and goals of the movement. This Disraeli did in the Young England trilogy which presents the religious, social, and political views of the Young England manifesto. They sought an organic society; and, like Carlyle before them and Ruskin after them, they turned their view to the past, the sense of which permeates Disraeli's thought and novels.

Reviewing the state of English and European historiography during the first decades of the nineteenth century, we can well understand Disraeli's interest in and use of historical motifs.[23] It is with his particular interpretation of the past, however, that my discussion deals. Disraeli's emphasis in his conception of history as an organic continuum lies in the sphere of religion. The great principles by which mankind must be moved can be discovered only by man's understanding and heeding the Law which Disraeli sees in the Hebraeo-Christian Church (which I discuss at some length in Chapter 5). Societal organization and governmental and political structures, although of tremendous importance in any hierarchical patterning of society, are at all times considered secular appendages of the Church: they are controlled ultimately by the Law as interpreted by the Church. This is, of course, the cardinal reason why so many medievally or, at least, traditionally oriented thinkers such as Burke, Carlyle, Coleridge, and Disraeli view the position of authority—secular or ecclesiastical—with such great reverence. The law-giver is, in reality, the Law-interpreter, and, as such, his task is awesome.

VII *Novelist: Extension of the Politician*

When John Holloway suggests that "Disraeli's novels . . . contain a pattern of enquiry typical of the moralist or seer raising 'ultimate' questions; and one must see how it is to these ultimate questions that his novels suggest an answer, not only to more circumscribed political issues,"[24] he raises a fundamental problem in Disraeli criticism. The primary reason that most Disraeli scholarship (excluding the biographical) fails to look beneath the word of the writer is that little attempt has been made to reconstruct the world-view which emerges from the novels.[25] That Disraeli is a satirist and a political novelist (a phrase, by the way, which still needs great qualification and study) is true. But Disraeli is much more than these things; and, by studying Disraeli's works against their ideological background, we can come closest to the essential Disraeli.

Disraeli was a great politician, but he was also an accomplished novelist. There are not—as some critics suggest—two Disraelis; instead, the novelist is an extension of the practicing politician. Through our attempt to isolate the writer's ideas as developed in his novels, the politician and the man should become better understood. But, and this point is crucial, the novels deal with more than politics, which, in any ultimate analysis, become the background for the greater ideas contained in the trilogy. It is in the line of such a depth-approach to Disraeli that John Holloway's unfortunately brief account becomes significant, for Holloway does raise some very significant points. He sees Carlyle's relationship to Disraeli; he comments upon Disraeli's use of the hero motif; and he recognizes Disraeli's organic concept of history. Although he develops none of these matters to any extent, Holloway is moving into what should become the mainstream of Disraeli scholarship.

It is important, therefore, to recognize at the outset that Disraeli was both a practicing politician and an imaginative writer and that his political ideas and literary efforts are of a piece. Two critics, Walter Allen and V. S. Pritchett, highlight this fact. Allen stresses that "as a novelist Disraeli's limitations were many and obvious. His strength lay in his specialized knowledge; it would be almost true to say he had to become a politician before he could become a novelist. But within his limitations he grasped and expressed the essential situation of his times with a boldness beyond that of much greater novelists."[26] "After a hundred years," says Pritchett,

how exactly Disraeli has defined the English political situation. He is our only political novelist; I mean, the only one *saturated* in politics; the only one whose intellect feasts on polity. Strikes, riots, questions of social justice, elections and backstairs politics enliven other Victorian novelists of the period frequently; but of Mrs. Gaskell, George Eliot, Meredith, Trollope it cannot be said that politics are their blood. These writers do not convert us to this view or that; they are cautious; they do not inflame us; on the whole they leave us with the impression that political action is a disagreeable duty, distracting us from the major interests of human nature. Children of a competitive society, heirs of the Utilitarians, they see politics as the indispensable but tedious regulator. Politics are a method, a humane technique of adjustment; and, in general, it must be said that this has been the English view throughout the nineteenth century and after. To Disraeli, the Jew and alien, such a theory was pragmatic and despicable.[27]

VIII *Determination for Greatness*

In Disraeli's early life we see existing side by side the seeds of egotism, self-assurance, ambition, brilliance, and romantic mysticism. There was no question in the young Benjamin's mind as to what type of person he wished to be—a great man. Even though the particular avenue toward this passionately desired goal was not to become clear for many years, he knew, when he did decide on politics, not only that he wanted to become Prime Minister, but that he would become Prime Minister. Once he had made his decision, Disraeli worked consciously and methodically toward that end. Until his marriage to the widowed Mary Anne Lewis, Disraeli posed as a dandy. Yet, even though he enjoyed the stance of dandyism, this role was completely contrived: one had to attract attention. Disraeli had public behavior schematized and blueprinted; for, in private, he was a different man. In this respect, he epitomizes the split personality so necessary to the man in public life. And, as a statesman, Disraeli was magnificent.

The fact that he had been born a Jew, coupled with his pride and feeling for Jewish history and tradition (rather than for Hebrew religion and ritual), was to handicap Disraeli in public life. His original religion was always considered a political liability by both friends and enemies. André Maurois states that after Disraeli's first ministry was formed, "there was at least one man in England in whose eyes this elevation of Disraeli, and this intimacy of the Crown with a Hebrew mountebank was an intolerable scandal: that was Mr. Gladstone."[28] And his was a common view among the opposition. Yet, Disraeli emerges as one of *the* statesmen of the age.[29]

Disraeli's other side, the imaginative writer, is more complex. In the world of politics and statecraft, Disraeli was constantly faced with expediency and compromise. In political maneuvering and in-fighting, ideals were tempered by a less than ideal reality; but, in his non-political life, Disraeli was able to drop the statesman's pose and to develop truer feelings and more essential ideas. In his non-political life, the imaginative writer could climb above the pressures and concerns of the moment to dwell in the past and, more important, in the future. He could give play to his ideals in terms of the imaginative world of his fictional creations. Certainly one major aspect of Disraeli's non-political existence is to be found in his literary creations which occupy that significant position between the public and private worlds of their author.

Disraeli is credited with having created the genre of the political novel in English. It is understandable that the world of politics should form the backdrop for his literary productions, for what world did he know better? But, since Disraeli is dealing

with a fictionalized, imaginative world (albeit one often based
on reality), he could portray politics and, indeed, the world order
itself any way he wished them to be. In his novels there was no
need to compromise his ideals. In the England created in his
imagination, men and institutions could coincide with his dreams
of men and their institutions. In his novels, therefore, we can
often perceive the ideologically uncompromised Disraeli. Moreover, for the student of the nineteenth century, the novels can
often illuminate the actions of the statesman; for the novelist's
imagination is always played off against the historical and political facts of the age. And the tension between imaginative and
historical fact is in Disraeli's novels always interesting and
generally illuminating.

CHAPTER 2

Early Novels: From Vivian Grey *to Young England*

A COMMON cliché about Disraeli claims that, although none of his novels is a work of genius, they are all works of a genius. The cliché may well be true. Even in Disraeli's minor novels there are to be found flashes of brilliant observation, witty dialogue, and incisive political or social commentary. Unfortunately, there are only a few novels in which any of the art of fiction is sustained. Disraeli is responsible for eleven novels, but his reputation as a novelist must rest finally, as we have noted, upon only three: *Coningsby, Sybil,* and *Tancred.* Yet in the early novels there are embedded many of the ideas which were later to be more fully developed.

Disraeli had mentioned in his diary that *Vivian Grey, Contarini Fleming,* and *Alroy* illustrate his own desires and feelings. While Disraeli thought *Contarini Fleming* indicated the development of his poetic sensibilities, he said that "in *Vivian Grey* I have portrayed my active and real ambition; in *Alroy* my ideal ambition." The autobiographical material implicit in the novels has been dealt with at length by others (most notably by Monypenny and Buckle) and, therefore, the reader can satisfy his curiosity elsewhere about this relationship.[1] My present interest is with the themes and ideas which run through the early novels and which look forward to the mature work. These early novels are the products of a fledgling writer not yet fully committed to serious writing and of a man who often created fiction in order to stave off his growing number of creditors. Their fundamental interest lies in that extra-literary area which sheds more light on the condition of the author than on the condition of man. Yet they are almost always interesting; and, since Disraeli's

Young England novels are important, his other productions take on the glow of reflected interest especially as they are related to the novels of the 1840's.

I Vivian Grey (1826-27)

Disraeli, writing in a preface to his works in 1853, said of *Vivian Grey*:

Books written by boys, which pretend to give a picture of manners, and to deal in knowledge of human nature, must necessarily be founded on affectation. They can be, at the best, but the results of imagination, acting upon knowledge not acquired by experience. Of such circumstances, exaggeration is a necessary consequence, and false taste accompanies exaggeration. Nor is it necessary to remark that a total want of art must be observed in their pages, for that is a failing incident to all first efforts. When the writers of such books are not again heard of, the works, even if ever noticed, are soon forgotten, and so there is no great harm done. But, when their authors subsequently become eminent, such works often obtain a peculiar interest, and are sought for from causes irrespective of their merits. Such productions should be exempt from criticism, and should be looked upon as a kind of literary lusus.

These observations apply to VIVIAN GREY. For more than a quarter of a century its author has refused to reprint it; but the action of the foreign presses in the present day, especially in the United States and Germany, renders an author no longer the master of his own will. It has, therefore, been thought best to include it in this general edition of his works, and so it is hoped that it will be read with an indulgent recollection of the conditions under which it was produced. (xxi)

It is small wonder that the Disraeli of 1853 would have preferred to forget the novel produced by the Disraeli of 1825. *Vivian Grey* is the story of a young and—we are told—brilliant man who possesses all save one of the necessary qualifications for leading his fellow men: he does not have the means of initiating his public career. Neither is his family titled or landed, nor has he the necessary aristocratic patrons; and in this lament of Vivian we come upon one of the recurring themes of the early novels. Over and over again, the reader is reminded of the great pain which must accompany talent without opportunity—the cry not only of Vivian Grey but of Contarini Fleming and of Alroy. Without question, it also expresses the innermost thoughts of the young Disraeli.

The explosion of popularity ignited by *Vivian Grey* was in an inverse ratio to its artistry. That the novel was a success with London society is perhaps the sharpest indicator of one aspect of the nature of that society and of the state of the English novel in the 1820's. *Vivian Grey* was launched by its publisher, Colburn, as the newest novel of fashionable life by an anonymous writer, and the implication was clear. Here was a novel written about society by a member of society who, for obvious reasons, preferred to keep his identity unknown. As a result, *Vivian Grey* became the season's great guessing game. Keys were prepared identifying the novel's characters, and Disraeli was now a member —albeit a silent one—of the literary fraternity. But if society had been taken in, not so William Jerdan of the *Literary Gazette,* who wrote that "the class of the author was a little betrayed by his frequent recurrence to topics about which the mere man of fashion knows nothing and cares less." Jerdan notwithstanding, however, the novel's sales and interest in *Vivian Grey* continued to mount until news of its authorship found its way into the public ear. The angry response was great; it was certainly far in excess of the crime. But society did not like being "taken in"— especially by an interloper, an alien. Disraeli's health broke; he decided to tour the Continent.

The trip was fortunate in that Disraeli's health was restored and a good number of interesting and highly descriptive travel letters were written to his sister. The trip was unfortunate, however, in that the second half of *Vivian Grey* grew out of it. If the first portion of the novel (originally published separately) has little to commend it, it is nevertheless masterly when contrasted with its concluding portion. Disraeli was obviously in need of money; the novel of fashionable life was popular; the publisher was more than willing; and so in 1826 a sequel to *Vivian Grey* was published. Again society embraced Vivian, but the work teeters on the edge of literary disaster. The consistency of the literary taste of London society, however, remained unimpaired.

Vivian Grey, the first lengthy work of a very young man, has a contrived and unconvincing plot; and it is, of course, notably autobiographical. What else does one generally write about— indeed, think about—at twenty-one? The portions of the novel dealing with society are the least effective since Disraeli knew nothing of society. (How different is the handling of the same subject in the novels from *Coningsby* on. Disraeli is then sure of his ability, for he describes and comments upon that which he has come to know and understand.) The autobiographical material moves revealingly and interestingly from Horace Grey as the imaginative counterpart of Isaac D'Israeli to Vivian's visit to Cleveland, which not only is drawn from Benjamin's mission to secure as editor of his daily J. G. Lockhart, son-in-law of Sir Walter Scott, but poignantly delivers the frustration and despair suffered by Disraeli when his own newspaper scheme—the *Representative* (1825)—collapsed.

However, what is more important in *Vivian Grey* is the hero's overwhelming desire for fame and power. This desire is important biographically, but it is also one of the necessary first stages in the development of Disraeli's hero motif which we will see brought to its development in the Young England trilogy. Although none of the philosophical or ideological framework is yet present, the early novels do present young men who sense that they are leaders and shapers of men and who desire to implement this realization. Although Vivian's enterprises fail and although he does not gain his dreamed-of political preferment, he does experience the momentary taste of power and success; and his appetite for both is sharpened. He can concur with Contarini Fleming's assessment of himself as possessing a great imagination but as being a mere boy, yet he also realizes the possibilities of the future.

The novel concludes with Vivian stranded in the midst of a storm and flood and with Disraeli apparently hard pressed for an ending. At this suspenseful moment, "Vivian's horse, with a maddened snort, dashed down the hill; his master, senseless, clung to his neck; the frantic animal was past all government; he stood upright in the air, flung his rider, and fell dead!" (519). With this conclusion to his novel's action, the young writer abandoned artistic integrity to the expedient concern of getting out from under his plot. After the horse's downhill bolt, the author intrudes:

Here we leave Vivian! It was my wish to have detailed, in the present portion of this work, the singular adventures which befell him in one of the delightful of modern cities, light hearted Vienna! But his history has expanded under my pen, and I fear that I have, even now, too much presumed upon an attention which I am not entitled to command. I am, as yet, but standing without the gate of the Garden of Romance. True it is, that as I gaze through the ivory bars of its Golden Portal, I would fain believe that, following my roving fancy, I might arrive at some green retreats hitherto unexplored, and loiter among some leafy bowers where none have lingered before me. But these expectations may be as vain as those dreams of Youth over which all have mourned. The disappointment of Manhood succeeds to the delusion of Youth: let us hope that the heritage of Old Age is not Despair. (520)

When asked, years later, what had happened to Vivian, Disraeli answered, "there was no inquest; Vivian Grey still lives." The response stands as one of Disraeli's best, but its real significance is not to be found on its literal level. Vivian Grey lived on, for in him we perceive the embryonic stage of the Disraelian hero. We might hazard the guess that it is in the young Disraeli himself that we perceive the elemental characteristics of the heroic being whose full portrait will later be delineated. Certainly the hero, in meaningful terms, is a product of the more mature author; only the impetus toward an undefined, perhaps unconscious, heroic motif is found in *Vivian Grey* and in other early novels.

After a close reading of the novel, we can well understand the seasoned author's preference to absolve himself of all responsibility for this book. In almost every sense, *Vivian Grey* is the product of a very young writer. We remember that about all Disraeli had to work with was a rough approximation of a plot and a sparse literary apprenticeship; he had almost no personal experience to draw upon. From this vantage point, we could be charitable. Yet the structure of the novel is so weak that the work can only limp to its conclusion. Furthermore, the novel is crammed with a variety of organically irrelevant digressions which must make the reader assume that the young novelist was intent on introducing any and all characters and episodes which he had stored up and which he felt were interesting. Chapter 15 of Book II, a good example, is nothing more than a fictional essay on the Toady. This is not to say that it is without interest or that it shows no ability; rather, it is to say that Disraeli was yet to learn the virtue of remaining in control of his work. This chapter epitomizes the structural weakness which the more sophisticated Disraeli generally overcame in the Young England trilogy in which almost all digressions are in some way organically functional in terms of plot and/or theme. In *Vivian Grey*, Disraeli is simply being clever as he insists on writing into the work what he considers "rich."

The novel is structurally immature and artistically provincial; but, perhaps, it is also simply youthful. In one of his many authorial intrusions,[2] Disraeli's rather casual attitude toward fiction is made manifestly plain: "These conversations play the very deuce with one's story. We had intended to have commenced this book with something quite terrific, a murder or a marriage; and all our great ideas have ended in a lounge. After all, it is, perhaps, the most natural termination" (153). We can smile at such blatant confusion of the fictive and real worlds, but we cannot be so polite in the presence of the sort of outlandish rhetoric the novelist employs when, for example, his young hero invokes the moon in a torrential, rhapsodic outpouring:

> O thou bright moon! thou object of my first love! thou shalt not escape an invocation, although perchance at this very moment some varlet sonnetteer is prating of 'the boy Endymion and 'thy silver bow.' Here to thee, Queen of the Night! in whatever name thou most delightest! Or Bendis, as they hailed thee in rugged Thrace; or Bubastis, as they howled to thee in mysterious Egypt; or Dian, as they sacrificed to thee in gorgeous Rome; or Artemis, as they sighed to thee on the bright plains of ever glorious Greece! Why is it that all men gaze on thee? Why is it that all men love thee? Why is it that all men worship thee? (115)

This incantation is followed by that weird and bacchanalian scene with Mrs. Felix Lorraine; a scene fraught with juvenile romanticism, a quasi-Germanic mysticism, and intimations of deeply psychotic behavior—a scene, by the way, that at its completion is simply consigned to limbo and is never brought back for either analysis or plot use. But—we might ask—why should it be resurrected? After all, the novel's strength is not plot. Even the death of Cleveland (in a duel with Vivian) exceeds the limits of verisimilitude: a "random" shot pierces Cleveland's heart! True, the novel has its full complement of structural flaws, unconvincing plot manipulations, and blatant narrative intrusions, but it is not without a certain interest. Its very popularity is a factor in behalf of its study by a literary sociologist as a curiosity. Its biographical data afford possibilities for better understanding Disraeli. Furthermore, there remain several problems involving this novel and Disraeli's later works.

Throughout *Vivian Grey* we encounter intimations of the later Disraeli. Even in this first novel, the author is often pithy, aphoristic, and witty; and he displays sparkling insight into people, politics, and institutions. Vivian, for example, "was too cunning a master of the human mind not to be aware of the quicksands upon which all greenhorns strike; he knew too well the danger of unnecessary intimacy. . . ." (39), or "he looked upon marriage as a comedy in which, sooner or later, he was, as a well paid actor, to play his part. . . ." (50). In the following passage, we encounter perhaps the rationalization underlying Disraeli's own pose of dandyism: "In England, personal distinction is the only passport to the society of the great. Whether this distinction arises from fortune, family, or talent, is immaterial; but certain it is, to enter into high society, a man must either have blood, a million, or a genius" (17).

And with refinement his later attacks certainly complement the assessment of the Marquess of Carabas' political position: "To compensate for his loss of office, and to secure his votes, the Earl of Carabas was promoted in the peerage, and was presented with some magnificent office, meaning nothing; swelling with dignity, and void of duties" (24). Disraeli's description of Mr. Toad's political ambiguity clearly looks forward to *Coningsby* and *Sybil*: "Mr. Toad's career in the House was as correct as his conduct out of it. After ten years' regular attendance, the boldest conjecturer would not have dared to define his political principles. It was a rule with Stapylton Toad never to commit himself" (72). His feeling for the mood of young aristocrats (before he became intimate with them) is later developed at the opening of *Sybil*.

"I think there is nothing more pleasant than talking over the season, in the country, in August."

"Nothing more agreeable. It was dull though, last season, very dull;

I think the game cannot be kept going another year. If it were not for the General Election, we really must have a war for variety's sake. Peace gets quite a bore. Everybody you dine with has a good cook, and gives you a dozen different wines, all perfect." (54-55)

The two most intriguing episodes in the novel involve John Conyers and Plato. John Conyers was a farmer who had aided Vivian in an encounter with a vicious horse. Two weeks after, however, Conyers (whom Vivian thought to be the model English husbandman) was reduced to total poverty and despair because his new master, not believing in credit for tenant farmers, had seized all of Conyers' possessions. The significant point is that Vivian goes out of his way to help Conyers. To be sure, the farmer had once helped Vivian; but after considering the nature of Disraeli's young protagonist, we must find this sympathetic act out of keeping with Vivian Grey's character. We remember that Vivian is frequently presented as an incipient Taper-Tadpole, a political opportunist who desires only pragmatic success. The assistance to Conyers is therefore structurally gratuitous. Perhaps, however, even in the Disraeli of twenty-one there is a vein of sympathy for the poor and oppressed. It is, of course, an untapped vein, but one which will in later years be heavily mined by the author.

Earlier in the novel, Vivian is caught up in the study of Plato:

Wonderful is it that while the whole soul of Vivian Grey seemed concentrated and wrapped in the glorious pages of the Athenian; while, with keen and almost inspired curiosity, he searched, and followed up, and meditated upon, the definite mystery, the indefinite development; while his spirit alternately bowed in trembling and in admiration, as he seemed to be listening to the secrets of the universe revealed in the glorious melodies of an immortal voice; wonderful is it, I say, that the writer, the study of whose works appeared to the young scholar, in the revelling of his enthusiasm, to be the sole object for which man was born and had his being, was the cause by which Vivian Grey was saved from being all his life a dreaming scholar. (14-15)

The hierarchical and historical principles inherent in the Young England trilogy point up the importance of this aspect of the young Disraeli's intellectual enthusiasm. Of greatest significance is the last portion of the statement in which we see Vivian moved from a life of dreaming scholarship to one of practical concerns by his involvement with Plato. This certainly sounds more like a Coningsby or an Egremont (the protagonist of *Sybil*) than a Vivian Grey. Thus this episode and the John Conyers affair, both out of keeping with the non-ideological tone of the novel, offer rich insight into the author.

Finally, we return to that "active and real ambition" which Disraeli claimed was presented in *Vivian Grey*. That his real ambition is one which must include political power and success is, of course, unquestionable. But that the conception of real ambition is open to a variety of qualifiers is also unquestionable. When any man talks of his three kinds of ambition, he cannot separate them completely; they must blend into one another and form alloys which obviously change as well as complicate the original entities. Disraeli does indeed speak of three kinds of ambition, but he cannot in fact present any one of them in a pure state. In *Vivian Grey*, for example, the active ambition is at the center of the stage, but it is not unaffected by the others. We perceive the same kind of commingling in the two other novels of the "biographical trilogy."

II The Young Duke (1831)

The Young Duke is more important than *Vivian Grey* in terms of Disraeli's later works, especially the Young England trilogy. Granted that the primary motivating factor behind the production of this novel was the need for money coupled with the success achieved by *Vivian Grey* only a few years before, *The Young Duke* nevertheless looks forward to the kind of educative process that the men of Young England experienced. That the protagonist's education stops short of any clearly articulated credo merely attests to the fact that neither the Duke nor Disraeli, in 1830, had as yet formulated one. It would be another five years before the publication of the *Vindication of the English Constitution* and fourteen years before the launching of the Young England novels. Yet Disraeli, in *The Young Duke*, begins to employ politics and contemporary social questions as he had not in either *Vivian Grey* or any of his short fiction prior to 1830.[3]

Disraeli, too, looked with greater approval at this novel than at its predecessor. His 1853 Advertisement is interesting:

The reader will be kind enough to recollect that THE YOUNG DUKE was written "when George the Fourth was King" (1829), nearly a quarter of a century ago, and that, therefore, it is entitled to the indulgence which is the privilege of juvenile productions. Though its pages attempt to pourtray the fleeting manners of a somewhat frivolous age, it is hoped that they convey a moral of a deeper and a more permanent character. Young authors are apt to fall into affectation and conceit, and the writer of this work sinned very much in these respects; but the affectation of youth should be viewed leniently, and every man has the right to be conceited until he is successful. (vii)

In one sense, of course, Disraeli refers to *The Young Duke* as a juvenile novel (essentially what he had said about *Vivian Grey*); but, after twenty-five years, the author still approves of the novel's moral which is of a "deeper and a more permanent character" than the age portrayed, the world of 1829. Indeed, the work's subtitle is *A Moral Tale, though Gay*; and the moral of this novel is developed in the growth of the protagonist.

The young Duke's début is representative of the nature of his life and of the atmosphere and tone of his class:

Easter was over, the sun shone, the world was mad, and the young Duke made his début at Almack's. He determined to prove that he had profited by a winter at Vienna. His dancing was declared consummate. He galloped with grace and waltzed with vigour. It was difficult to decide which was more admirable, the elegance of his prance or the precision of his whirl. (23)

We need only to compare this protagonist at twenty-one with Coningsby, Egremont, and Tancred to see the distance between Young England and their fellows. The Duke is precisely what was expected of the young aristocracy. He was "flung forth, like the rest of his golden brethren, to corrupt the society of which he was the brightest ornament" (17).

And he was the brightest ornament only because it was his turn to take center stage: he was rich and newly arrived at his majority. Soon another "brightest ornament" would arrive, but at this moment the Duke was it; and "From this hour he delivered himself up to a sublime selfishness. With all his passions and all his profusion, a callousness crept over his heart. His sympathy for those he believed his inferiors and his vassals was slight. Where we do not respect we soon cease to love; when we cease to love, virtue weeps and flies. His soul wandered in dreams of omnipotence" (36). But here—early in the novel—the narrator intrudes to set the tone for the greater drama which the novel is to contain: "This picture perhaps excites your dislike; perchance your contempt. Pause! Pity him! Pity his fatal youth!"

This narrative comment immediately creates a tension between the life being described and the reader's realization of the author's reading of that life. Further, a biographical tension is created between the author's own desires (as extrapolated from *Vivian Grey,* for example) and his intellectualized estimate of at least a portion of those desires. Thus there is a fascination to be had in witnessing young Disraeli condemn a way of life which he yearns for and, at the same time, reject that way of life as he takes halting, tentative steps toward an as yet undefined greater commitment. In these terms, it is significant to survey the factors of the tension.

One of the charges Disraeli constantly levels at the young aristocracy is that it is engaged in a bootless chase after pleasure and, in that process, engages in a conspicuous consumption which ultimately produces only *ennui.* The aristocracy, interested only in self-gratification, fears nothing more than boredom. Even in this early novel Disraeli perceives this flaw:

He [the young Duke] had promised to spend a week with Charles Annesley and Lord Squib, who had taken some Norfolk Baronet's seat for the autumn, and while he was at Spa were thinning his preserves. It *was* a week! What fantastic dissipation! One day the brains of three hundred hares made a *pâté* for Charles Annesley. Oh, Heliogabalus! You gained eternal fame for what is now done in a corner! (51)

The great fête at the Pavilion (Book III, Chapter 10) and the dinner at the Alhambra (Chapter 18) also demonstrate the quest for pleasure and the desire for the means to further that quest. In May's theatrical, even the women are rigid and bored (108-12). Ultimately, Disraeli describes such an existence in the metaphor of disease, for this dull and weary seeking after excitement must quickly exhaust the possibilities of it. A new object is always necessary, and new objects become more and more scarce: "But when the splendour is discovered to be monotony; the change, order, and the caprice, a system; when the characters play ever the same part, and the variety never varies; how dull, how weary, how infinitely flat, is such a world to that man who requires . . . constant excitement!" (237). Finally, as it must, the quest becomes more frenzied and more nearly impossible: "The Young Duke appointed Lord Squib master of the ceremonies, and gave orders for nothing but constant excitement" (239).

What is important here is that both the Duke and Disraeli— unlike most of the Duke's peers—are aware of the futility and destructiveness of this debilitating way of life; and this awareness in 1830 far outshadows the fact that no viable alternatives are yet present. When the Duke despairs of his condition and speaks of virtue and duty, he is acknowledging not only a major change in himself but the possibility of change in all aristocrats. From the moment of this realization ("We cannot work without a purpose and an aim"), it is not long before the Duke becomes distressed and then disgusted with his associates (251); and he finally comes to describe his world as "this Babylon." As if acknowledging the negative education which he has received, the Duke laments: "I may never know what happiness is, but I think I know what happiness is not. It is not the career which I have hitherto pursued" (268).

This change, again, is a rather remarkable one for Disraeli to engineer. For even though there are distinct analogues between the growth of the Duke and that of the members of Young England, there are at the same time some very sharply contrasting notions in this novel—as in the following narrative comments:

My friends! What a blunder is youth! Ah! Why does truth light her torch but to illumine the ruined temple of our existence! Ah! Why do we know we are men only to be conscious of our exhausted energies! (87)

For I am one, though young, yet old enough to know ambition is a demon; and I fly from what I fear. (88)

A want of tact is worse than a want of virtue. (99)

[40]

No doubt, we can ascribe these comments to the youth of the novelist, but they demonstrate also the changes which occur in Disraeli's young men and narrators as well as in the author. Fundamentally, the major change involves awareness of self and society, a change which the narrator suggests late in *The Young Duke*:

Before a man can address a popular assembly with command, he must know something of mankind; and he can know nothing of mankind without knowing something of himself. Self-knowledge is the property of that man whose passions have their play, but who ponders over their results. Such a man sympathises by inspiration with his kind. He has a key to every heart. He can divine, in the flash of a single thought, all that they require, all that they wish. Such a man speaks to their very core. (307)

We might suggest also that in this passage Disraeli delineates one of the characteristics of the hero which he fully articulates in the Young England novels. These novels are broader and richer in scope than *Vivian Grey* and *The Young Duke* which Disraeli keeps at only one level—that of the careless, frivolous, gratification-seeking aristocrats. The author's own vision is not yet broadened as a writer or as a man. The social, political, and economic turmoil of *Coningsby, Sybil,* and *Tancred* belongs literally to another world or, in Disraeli's terms, to another nation. Although the Duke comes to distrust his world, his alternatives have been limited because of his total immersion in it. Thus, although there is hope for the Duke, his future can be described only in the general and romantically exaggerated terms which Disraeli chooses to close the novel.

I have suggested that Disraeli, in *The Young Duke,* first begins to make use of politics and contemporary social questions and that he does so while the novel as a whole remains geared to only one level of presentation. There are several moments at which we catch glimpses of the world beyond the limits of the Duke's *milieu,* and these are significant in terms of Disraeli's developing awareness. In *Vivian Grey* there was but the single moment of farmer John Conyers; in *The Young Duke* there are at least a half dozen such moments: the Duke's realization of "great agricultural distress" (269) which is brought home to him in the hard terms of dollars and cents; his visit to the tenant cottagers (291 ff);[4] the meeting with Mrs. Burnet, his aid to her, and the tacit acknowledgement of real human problems (322-23); the Duke's speech during the Catholic debate (327-28); and his knowledge of the sharp attacks from anti-aristocrats (321 ff). Of these, the last two subjects recur throughout the novel.

The young novelist displays an ambivalent attitude toward Catholics in his novel. On the one hand, he treats them with ironic humor; on the other, he praises them warmly. Perhaps he has not yet come to a clearly defined attitude toward Catholics, but this novel marks the beginning of a continuing and generally sympathetic interest in the Roman Catholic Church. Not only does the Duke marry May Dacre, a Roman Catholic, but we find several references in the novel to the Catholic past and to pride in ancestry. The other recurring motif involves the anti-aristocrats who are presented as Utilitarians who deliver their exaggerated opinions in "scholarly" articles in their distinguished journal, *The Screw and Lever Review*. The novelist is severe in his satire and firm in his conviction that the aristocracy must prevail (ultimately, of course, with the refinements delineated in later works rather than the glib and unconvincing position of this novel's last two paragraphs). Finally, of course, in the broad conception of the two novels, there is a greater general awareness of society in *The Young Duke* than in *Vivian Grey*.

The second novel is structurally sounder than the first, although the narrator is still allowed to take liberties which underscore the author's youth: "But to our tale. If we be dull, skip" (47); or "We really have had so many balls in this and other as immortal works that, in a literary point of view, we think we must give up dancing" (81); or "O, ye immortal gods! Nothing so difficult as to begin a chapter, and therefore have we flown to you. . . . After a paragraph or so our blood is up . . ." (267).[5] The liberties are less frequent, however, and the irrelevant episodes less obtrusive than in *Vivian Grey*. Furthermore, in this novel Disraeli, apparently self-conscious about his role as writer and having thought about that role, devotes some time to a discussion of the novel of "refined society." He presents both his reading of the standard formula and his own method which he maintains is different from that formula:

It is said that the conduct of refined society, in a literary point of view, is, on the whole, productive but of slight interest; that all we can aspire to is, to trace a brilliant picture of brilliant manners; and that when the dance and the festival have been duly inspired by the repartee and the sarcasm, and the gem, the robe, and the plume adroitly lighted up by the lamp and lustre, our cunning is exhausted. And so your novelist generally twists this golden thread with some substantial silken cord, for use, and works up, with the light dance, and with the heavy dinner, some secret marriage, and some shrouded murder. And thus, by English plots and German mysteries, the page trots on, or jolts, till, in the end, Justice will have her way, and the three volumes are completed.

A plan both good, antique, and popular, but not our way. We prefer trusting to the slender incidents which spring up from out our common intercourse. There is no doubt that that great pumice-stone, Society, smooths down the edges of your thoughts and manners. Bodies of men who pursue the same object must ever resemble each other: the life of the majority must ever be imitation. Thought is a labour to which few are competent; and truth requires for its development as much courage as acuteness. So conduct becomes conventional, and opinion is a legend; and thus all men act and think alike. (240-41)

These remarks are relevant in terms of Disraeli's 1853 Advertisement for the novel. The young novelist has maintained that all men are finally alike, and the implication must be that his novel deals not simply with refined society but with all society. Apparently after twenty-three years Disraeli still held this view, for he maintained that the "moral" of *The Young Duke* was deep and permanently significant. His reading of the wasted and spent young aristocrats remained consistent through the Young England trilogy. Most important, however, is the fact that in 1830 Disraeli was giving some articulated thought to the writing of fiction although he was not yet aware of the didactic possibilities of the art—ones which he consciously exploits in the trilogy.[6]

III   Contarini Fleming (1832)

Contarini Fleming, a sad, almost melancholy novel, not only differs in this sense from those works which preceded it but is more mature, although not necessarily more successful. However, the fact is that for about the first three-quarters of the book

Disraeli rises to the best work of his young career (and, excluding the disastrous concluding quarter of the novel, the best fiction before *Coningsby*). It was in *Contarini Fleming* that Disraeli claimed to have presented his poetic ambition, and the novel is heavily autobiographical. In the six years between *Vivian Grey* and this novel, Disraeli had learned much about the craft of fiction and about his own complicated and often polar desires. Where Vivian knew that he wanted political power, Contarini is torn between public life and art. This tension Disraeli manipulates effectively while offering a wide range of motifs which are developed in more significant terms in the Young England novels. In a variety of ways, therefore, *Contarini Fleming* is a meaningful early novel for a better understanding of the later works and of Disraeli himself.

There is obviously much of Disraeli reflected in the youth of Contarini Fleming, a sensitive child who needed and sought the assurance of love. His early education bears striking resemblances to Disraeli's own as Contarini's parents' concerns about their son's schooling parallel those of the author's. At school, the first intimations of the later tension between art and public life manifest themselves. Contarini's initial response to his new schoolfellows is a sudden determination to control them: "Did I tremble? Did I sink into my innermost self? Did I fly? Never. As I gazed upon them, a new principle rose up in my breast, and I perceived only beings whom I was determined to control"(23). This determination is coupled with a powerful ambition to form one element in the tension which will ultimately torture the protagonist. It is also at school that Contarini is first captivated by the music of language and by the desire to write: "For the first time in my life I composed. I grew intoxicated with my own eloquence. A new desire arose in my mind, novel aspirations which threw light upon old and often-experienced feelings. I began to ponder over the music of language; I studied the collocation of sweet words, and constructed elaborate sentences in lonely walks" (27). The problem of reconciling these two motivating forces becomes one of the novel's central interests.

Contarini does indeed write; and his novel *Manstein* and its reception are obviously drawn from Disraeli's rueful memories of *Vivian Grey*. After several abortive attempts at writing, Contarini is finally able to complete a novel (and in only seven days). He thought *Manstein* vigorous although he was able to say about it that ". . . it was altogether a most crude performance, teeming with innumerable faults. It was entirely deficient in art" (165). Almost everything which Contarini says and thinks about *Manstein*, Disraeli must have said and thought about *Vivian Grey*; but, like the young Disraeli, the young Contarini has the novel published and is launched into anonymous fame. *Manstein* quickly became the most talked-of book in society, and the identity of its author was society's most interesting guessing game. Two months after publication, the "great critical journal of the north of Europe" reviewed *Manstein*, and Disraeli undoubtedly understood too well Contarini's response to that destructive review:

With what horror, with what blank despair, with what supreme, appalling astonishment, did I find myself, for the first time in my life, a subject of the most reckless, the most malignant, and the most adroit ridicule. I was sacrificed, I was scalped. They scarcely condescended to notice my dreadful satire; except to remark, in passing, that, by-the-bye, I appeared to be as ill-tempered as I was imbecile. But all my eloquence, and all my fancy, and all the strong expression of my secret feelings! These ushers of the court of Apollo fairly laughed me off Parnassus, and held me up to public scorn, as exhibiting a lamentable instance of mingled pretension and weakness, and the most ludicrous specimen of literary delusion that it had ever been their unhappy office to castigate, and, as they hoped, to cure. (182)

Later in life, Contarini says of *Manstein* essentially what Disraeli had said of *Vivian Grey*: "If there were anything in the world for which I now entertained a sovereign contempt, it was my unfortunate *Manstein!* My most malignant critic must have yielded to me the scorn which I lavished on that immature production, and the shame with which I even recollected its existence" (259).

This entire *Manstein* motif in *Contarini Fleming* is particularly telling, for in it we can perceive Disraeli's growing sophistication about his writing. Just as Contarini continued to write after *Manstein* (indeed, felt compelled to do so), Disraeli continued to write and to become increasingly self-conscious about his work. By no means am I suggesting that Disraeli ever became a polished craftsman, but he obviously achieves a sense of structure and narrative propriety which we can observe developing from the earliest novels through the novels of the 1840's. We imagine that Contarini's method of composition after *Manstein* was essentially Disraeli's; he wrote rapidly, almost ecstatically, and in violation of his previously and carefully designed plans: "I prepared myself for composition in a very different mood from that in which I had poured forth my fervid crudities in the garden-house [when writing *Manstein*]. Calm and collected, I constructed characters on philosophical principles, and mused over a chain of action. . . . All was art" (259-60). Only after this careful outline had been completed did Contarini begin to write: "I began to write; my fancy fired, my brain inflamed; breathing forms rose up under my pen, and jostled aside the cold abstractions, whose creation had cost such long musing. In vain I endeavoured to compose without enthusiasm; in vain I endeavoured to delineate only what I had preconceived; in vain I struggled to restrain the flow of unbidden invention" (260).

Throughout Disraeli's novel Contarini is, of course, involved with his father's political activities. When, as a young boy, Contarini saw for the first time his father at his office (Secretary of State for Foreign Affairs), he was struck by the greatness of the Baron's position and power: "I began to muse upon this idea of political greatness" (97). From this moment in the novel, Contarini is moved into a political career, first as his father's secretary and later as Undersecretary for Foreign Affairs while his father is Prime Minister. The irony of Contarini's life is not only that public service satisfies many of his deepest desires for power over his fellows but that he is extraordinarily effective in his political duties. Yet even in the flush of diplomatic victory, Contarini longs to create beautiful things. He had just broken a diplomatic impasse which neither his father nor his sovereign had been able to handle: "And as I gazed upon the sunset, and the star, and the dim beauties of the coming eve, my mind grew calm, and all the bravery of my late reverie passed away. And I felt indeed a disgust for all the wordliness on which I had been late pondering. And there arose in my mind a desire to create things beautiful as that golden sun and that glittering star" (173).

The protagonist is thus literally caught between two powerful motivating forces, each contending for his future and each offering him the possibility of influencing men. The Baron, believing that his son will one day "be Prime Minister . . . perhaps something greater," obviously urges a career of public service. Earlier, the Baron had discussed the relative merits of the active as opposed to the poetic life. He believed that great poets were in their lifetime "the most miserable of their species"; they were "depressed, doubtful, obscure"; "often unappreciated, utterly uninfluential, beggars, flatterers of men unworthy even of their recognition" (151). Contarini's father insisted that a man of ambition and talent must have fame during his own lifetime rather than after; posthumous fame, he told Contarini, is a mockery: "We are active beings, and our sympathy, above all other sympathies, is with great action" (152). Contarini's ultimate problem is attempting to discover the lever—poetry or politics— by which he can involve himself with great action. As we shall see at the novel's conclusion, Contarini decides upon a course not very unlike that which Disraeli himself was to elect. On the way to that conclusion, many indicators of the later novels are unfolded in the book.

In *Contarini Fleming* Disraeli first introduces the Sidonia-like teacher and sage, in this case the painter Peter Winter. The author treats Winter in a much more obvious manner than he later does Sidonia (in the Young England trilogy); but the artist's influence upon Contarini is of the same kind. Even the meeting between Contarini and Winter bears a striking resemblance to the initial meeting between Coningsby and Sidonia: both meetings take place in rustic surroundings; in each case the protagonist is immediately fascinated by the stranger; in neither case do the characters exchange names; and, of course, in both cases the men soon meet again. That the second meeting between Winter and Contarini is coincidental (and palpably contrived) not only offers another parallel between Winter and Sidonia but introduces the reader to what will become a persistent leitmotif in Disraeli's work: the power of destiny.

At the conclusion of the first meeting, Contarini was about to tell Winter his name when the artist stopped him and said, "I never wish to know anybody's name. Were I to become acquainted with every being who flits across me in life, the callousness of my heart would be endangered. If your acquaintance be worth preserving, fate or fortune will someday bring us again together" (56). Yet the effect of the moment with the stranger was great on Contarini: "It was strange the ascendancy that this man exercised over me. When he spoke I seemed listening to an oracle, and now that he had departed, I felt as if some supernatural visitant had disappeared" (56). Fate, indeed, becomes a real character in this novel as coincidental and mysterious events echo Winter's words on the subject. (Certainly the atmosphere surrounding Contarini's relationship with Alcesté, for example, is fraught with elements of unfolding destiny.)

Winter appears in the novel generally at critical moments in Contarini's development, and by his easy advice helps move Contarini through them: early in the novel it is Winter who sends the young Fleming home after he had run away; late in the novel it is Winter who prescribes a cure for Contarini's illness after physicians had been stymied for a year; and at the end of the novel it is Winter who moves Contarini to action and creation. If there is a shaping force in the protagonist's life, it is obviously Peter Winter. This artist manipulates the tension between art and public life so that Contarini is able to reach some sense of balance and to remove himself from the agony of being buffeted by unharmonized, discordant desires. Thus the device of Sidonia, a super-character who providentially aids a deserving protagonist, is first introduced in *Contarini Fleming*.

Disraeli's interest in Roman Catholicism and in the past is also expanded in this novel. The hero marries a Catholic girl in *The Young Duke*, but the protagonist himself converts to Roman Catholicism in *Contarini Fleming*. Yet the love for the past and the Church which motivates Contarini is of a qualitatively different kind from that devotion to the past which we shall see experienced by Young England. Contarini is taken with the trappings of tradition rather than with the ethos of either the Church or the past:

Many tall white candles, in golden sticks, illuminated the sacred table, redolent of perfumes and adorned with flowers. Six large burnished lamps were suspended above, and threw a magical light upon a magical picture. It was a Magdalen kneeling and weeping in a garden. Her long golden hair was drawn off her ivory forehead, and reached to the ground. Her large blue eyes, full of ecstatic melancholy, pierced to heaven, while the heavy tears studded like pearls her wan but delicate cheek. Her clasped hands embraced a crucifix.

I gazed upon this pictured form with a strange fascination. I came forward, and placed myself near the altar. At that moment the organ burst forth, as if heaven were opening; clouds of incense rose and wreathed around the rich and vaulted roof; the priest advanced, and revealed a God, which I fell down and worshipped. From that moment I became a Catholic. (46-47)

The point at hand is that the author's interest in both Roman Catholicism and the past emerges as a continuing one.

Disraeli's analysis of the wasted young aristocracy also continues in this novel. Between the time that Contarini first meets Winter and the young man departs for the university a striking change occurs in him. From an innocent, unaffected, fresh boy, Contarini is made to fit into the pattern of the young Duke's peers: ". . . at the age of fifteen I had unexpectedly become one of the most affected, conceited, and intolerable atoms that ever peopled the sunbeam of society" (112). Contarini was processed and packaged; and through Contarini's own detestation of what refined society expects a young man to be and to do, the reader appreciates a more oblique attack on the very aristocratic characteristics so frontally assaulted by Disraeli in his preceding novel. In addition to the melodrama it offers, the Secret Union for the Amelioration of Society, which Contarini organizes while at the university, underscores the novel's criticism of young aristocrats. Only after Contarini has struck out independently against his class and institution and only after he has been genuinely excited by the spirit of learning can he even contemplate so subversive an activity as the Secret Union.

Above all else, *Contarini Fleming* is interesting to the student of Disraeli, for we have in this novel the opportunity of observing the author's confused questioning of both past and future. In the early 1830's Disraeli is not so sure of the efficacy of the past as he was to become in the 1840's or, even a few short years later, in the *Vindication of the English Constitution*. In the last chapters of the novel, Disraeli has Contarini reflect on the past and future in a fitful and often contradictory fashion. These reflections are nearly all resolved in the Young England novels, once again indicating the growth and crystallization of Disraeli's outlook. Disraeli, only forty pages from the close of *Contarini Fleming*, has his protagonist comment in these terms:

Whatever may have been the faults of the ancient governments, they were in closer relation to the times, to the countries, and to the governed, than ours. The ancients invented their governments according to their wants; the moderns have adopted foreign policies, and then modelled their conduct upon this borrowed regulation. This circumstance has occasioned our manners and our customs to be so confused, and absurd, and unphilosophical. What business had we, for instance, to adopt the Roman law, a law foreign to our manners, and consequently disadvantageous? He who profoundly meditates upon the situation of Modern Europe will also discover how productive of misery has been the senseless adoption of oriental customs by northern people. Whence came that divine right of kings, which has deluged so many countries with blood? (320-21)

Ten pages later, Contarini meditates on the course of societies, historically and politically:

Is there then no hope? Is it an irrevocable doom, that society shall be created only to be destroyed? When I can accept such a dogma, let me also believe that the beneficent Creator is a malignant demon. Let us meditate more deeply; let us at length discover that no society can long subsist that is based upon metaphysical absurdities. The law that regulates man must be founded on a knowledge of his nature, or that law leads him to ruin. What is the nature of man? In every clime and in every creed we shall find a new definition. (331)

Here Contarini sounds like a cross between the Utilitarian and the new Tory conservative. Yet a few pages farther we find the following curiously antithetical remark: "Singular fate of modern ages, that beneficent Omnipotence has willed that for all our knowledge we should be indebted to the most insignificant of ancient states. Our divine instruction is handed down to us by an Arabian tribe . . ." (349). Which of these views is behind the novel's closing hopes for the protagonist's future is an interesting and perhaps moot question.[7] Once again, however, we have here the evidence for Disraeli's interests in the 1830's which bear fruit in the novels of the 1840's. There was to take place between 1832 and 1845 a considerable ripening of ideas which we shall see presented in the Young England novels.

I began this discussion of *Contarini Fleming* by suggesting that for the first three-quarters of his book Disraeli wrote his best fiction prior to *Coningsby*. In the unfortunate last quarter of the novel, Peter Winter's prescription for the ailing Contarini is travel, through which he would not only be cured but would find himself able to write once again. From the beginning of Part V, therefore, the reader is subjected to Contarini's year of travel. Disraeli was plot-ridden here and, instead of plot, can give us only travelogue. This travelogue quality (much like the esthetic and structural sin of the sequel to *Vivian Grey*) is the novel's most severe handicap. There is little organic function served by the cameo accounts of various European scenes which fill these pages. Disraeli, for example, describes Spain from the bull fight to the siesta, from Mediterranean sea breezes to Spanish women's expertness with fans. We are presented with bits of history and geography as Contarini's travels gradually become the reader's travail. It goes on—from Spain to Asia Minor. There are included—to break the monotony perhaps—short expository essays (Chapter 21 on education, for example) which are simply grosser intrusions in the midst of this structural confusion. Thus a rather good novel is unalterably crippled by its author's attempt to defeat an impossible plot situation. Yet Books I-IV, which hold up better than anything Disraeli had attempted before, offer intimations of plot control which Disraeli finally demonstrates in the Young England trilogy.

IV Alroy (1833)

The significance of *Alroy* to the later Young England novels is threefold. First, in this novel Disraeli most clearly articulates his debt to the past. Second, *Alroy* removes whatever doubt might have remained in any reader's mind about Disraeli's Hebraic consciousness. Third, and most important, is what will be discussed as the allegory of the novel—an allegory which develops the efficacy of great, traditional principles and of the destruction inherent in compromising them.

Much confusion has been engendered by Disraeli's comment

that his ideal ambition can be seen in *Alroy*. Monypenny has suggested that Disraeli was simply too astute a politician ever to have undertaken a Hebrew crusade. Philip Guedalla has commented that ". . . it is not easy to believe that he [Disraeli] ever played, even in fancy, with the notion of a Jewish career. Can we forget that *Contarini's* Jerusalem was largely notable for its Christian and Moslem antiquities? And even in *Alroy*, for all its highly scented eloquence, the Jewish quality was distinctly tepid."[8] Both Monypenny and Guedalla are essentially correct in their assumption that Disraeli never seriously considered a "Jewish career," but Disraeli's "ideal ambition" can be discussed in terms meaningful beyond the obviously limiting qualification of such a career. I have previously commented that Disraeli was emotionally and intellectually involved with the Hebrew "race" rather than with the Jewish religion, and in *Alroy* we have the clearest example of that involvement. Disraeli frequently goes to the past to discover (or uncover) traditional principles by which contemporary problems might be better understood and controlled. Is it not possible to read the author's ideal ambition in these terms as a commitment to traditional principles and to the Hebraic past? And, by Disraeli's own qualification, the Hebraic past must also include Christian tradition.

Furthermore, the diary entry in which he mentioned the ideal ambition reflected in *Alroy* was written in the same year that saw the publication of his *Vindication of the English Constitution* (1835). This is a Disraeli in his early thirties who is studiously engaged in a consideration of the past and who is also seriously intent on a political career. Yet he later looks back across the few years to *Alroy* and perceives his ideal ambition mirrored there. The commitment to tradition which permeates the *Vindication* might very well be part and parcel of Disraeli's reading of his ideal ambition in 1835. Furthermore, if we read *Alroy* in terms of the over-all pattern of thought in the Young England trilogy, the earlier novel must take on considerable ideational significance.

David Alroy and his career have symbolic value in terms of both the *Vindication* and the Young England novels. In its simplest terms, Alroy's mission is to deliver his people to their rightful position as tradition has defined that position. Alroy's quest is, in one sense, predicated upon his ability to invoke principles both by which his people's condition can be ameliorated and by which they can once more be brought into harmony with tradition. Essentially, of course, this is the mission of Young England and, in part, the intellectual proposition of the *Vindication*. Early in the novel, the clash between the proponent of the *status quo* (old Bostenay) and the advocate of a return to traditional greatness (paradoxically, therefore, of progress) sets the scene for Alroy's drama. Bostenay is able to admit that "we have fallen on evil days, and yet we prosper" (4), and, later, that "If life were a mere question between freedom and slavery, glory and dishonour, all could decide" (5). He urges acceptance of the present situation and denies Alroy's comments as the dreams of youth.

David, however, is seized by the realization that acquiescing to the present is not what he can or must do, although he remains uncertain about any precise course of action: "I know not what I feel, yet what I feel is madness. Thus to be is not to live, if life be what I sometimes dream, and dare to think it might be. To breathe, to feed, to sleep, to wake and breathe again, again to feel existence without hope; if this be life, why then these brooding thoughts that whisper death were better?" (8). This sounds very much like the young Coningsby or Egremont who realizes that he must engage change and embrace principles but is without a clear direction to follow. Indeed, the conversation between Bostenay and David bears resemblances to a dialogue between the old and new Toryism.[9] Even the songs sung by the chorus of Hebrew maidens are applicable to the new Toryism; for example: "THE BRICKS ARE FALLEN, BUT WE WILL REBUILD WITH MARBLE: THE SYCAMORES ARE CUT DOWN, BUT WE WILL REPLACE THEM WITH CEDARS" (15).

When David Alroy emerges as the deliverer of his people, he is aided by the mystical, Cabalistic Jabaster, who is the Sidonia-like teacher. He is able to bring David into contact with the great principles of the past and to channel his zeal into programs which offer some possibilities for success. Jabaster refers to David as his pupil, and states that he has mused "o'er his [Alroy's] future life . . . with a prophetic hope" (29). Throughout the novel, the influence of Jabaster on Alroy is paramount, even during those months when Alroy violates his master's counsel. Immediately after leaving Jabaster's cave, the young deliverer's adventures begin. He is seeking the sword of King Solomon through which he shall receive divine aid and which in itself is symbolic of the principles of tradition. Over and over again, David is rescued during his journey; and in every case he is saved by means of his religion. Furthermore he is guided and aided by a wide variety of mysterious as well as mystical occurrences.[10] In my reading of the novel as allegory, David is protected by his belief in great principles. And as long as his belief in those principles remains firm and unaltered, Alroy is successful. Only after he decides to compromise his original dedication does he fall from favor and meet with failure.

If Jabaster and David (during his quest) are representative of the dedication to traditional, efficacious principles, Schirene must be emblematic of the bed-and-board compromise which produces only boredom and isolation in the midst of a life of material luxury. She is neither happy nor even satisfied in the sumptuous, easy life she leads. Honain, on the other hand, the rationalist brother of Jabaster, is concerned only with the problem of surviving well. Perhaps a distant ancestor of Dickens' Gradgrind, Honain is interested only in demonstrable facts as he sells himself for comfort and power. His only allegiance is to those mortal powers which can make him prosperous and secure (whether those powers be Hebrew, Moslem, or Karasmian). Committed to the principle of self, he thinks his brother deluded.

To Alroy, both Schirene and Honain offer power and success without the "nonsense" of ideological commitment: "The world is before you. You may fight, you may love, you may revel. War, and women, and luxury are all at your command. With your person and talents you may be grand vizir. Clear your head of nonsense" (62). Alroy, a young man, is taken with these possibilities, especially with the beauty of Schirene; but he is also a pilgrim and realizes that he must continue his quest. His note to Honain makes clear the extent of the temptation he experienced: "Honain, I have been the whole night like David in the wilderness of Ziph; but, by the aid of the Lord, I have conquered. I fly from this dangerous city upon his business, which I have

too much neglected" (77). Yet this is precisely the city to which
Alroy will eventually return once he decides to alter and adapt
the principles of tradition. Once again, the Schirene-Honain view
of an uncommitted but prosperous life affords interesting parallels to the Young England conception of the old Toryism.

The change which Alroy undergoes is carefully wrought by
Disraeli. Through the early portions of the novel, the protagonist
is able to operate successfully while balancing practical action
on the one hand and commitment to principle on the other. From
his early dialogue with Bostenay, we perceive Alroy as a man
of action; from his first meeting with Jabaster, we perceive Alroy
as a man of commitment. Jabaster, too, realizes the need for
such a balance although he himself has lived in hermit-like,
mystical isolation, apparently only awaiting the arrival of the
deliverer. In this balance between action and commitment there
are intimations of the later outlook of Sidonia and the men of
Young England. We might suggest also that this is the relationship between action and thought which was operative in Disraeli's own career—or, at least, in his own ideal rendering of that
career. Clearly, then, there are two possible dangers inherent in
such a state of equilibrium: the balance can be upset by either
of the two elements gaining greater weight. Disraeli treats both
possibilities in this novel and rejects both.

After Alroy has left Jabaster's cave and has begun his search
for the sword, he listens to a debate between two learned rabbis
regarding the whereabouts of the weapon. The contrast between
the scholarly, rabbinic argument and Alroy's need and desire
for action is clear. Ultimately, the reader comes to recognize the
rabbis' dialogue to be sterile, meaningless prattle. Indeed, ex-
tolling the virtues of a learned treatise, one rabbi declares "the
first chapter makes equal sense, read backward or forward" (84).
Clearly, Disraeli intimates, no progress can ever arise from such
rarefied nonsense. Even Jabaster suggests that "the past is for
wisdom, the present for action, but for joy the future" (131).
However, although Alroy properly recoils from the rabbis, he
gradually moves to a position in which he finally states: "I'll
have no dreamers in authority. I must have practical men about
me, practical men" (147). From this rejection of tradition, it is
only a short movement to "The world is mine: and shall I yield

the prize . . . to realize the dull tradition of some dreaming priest, and consecrate a legend?" (148)

From this point of departure from tradition and principle, Alroy begins his downward turn to final ruin and capture by the Karasmians. Symbolically, as we shall see in the Young England trilogy, a marriage joins two opposing forces; but in this case destruction instead of strength is the result. Alroy is joined with Schirene; commitment is wedded to compromise. The offspring must be ruin for the committed, suggests the novel, as Alroy embraces compromise and conciliation in order to become the secular conqueror of the world in direct violation of the religious basis of his crusade. Jabaster's plea to Alroy to reject Schirene and all she represents is essentially what Alroy was able to convince himself of after first having met Schirene and Honain:

> Arise, Alroy, arise and rouse thyself. The lure that snared thy fathers may trap thee, this Delilah may shear thy mystic locks. Spirits like thee act not by halves. Once fall out from the straight course before thee, and, though thou deemest 'tis but to saunter mid the summer trees, soon thou wilt find thyself in the dark depths of some infernal forest, where none may rescue thee! (163)

But Alroy's dedication and commitment have been altered and sullied by success and power.[11]

While preparing to counter-attack the numerous, massive military invasions against him, Alroy realizes that changes have taken place: neither he nor his soldiers are fired by zeal and commitment as they had been previously, the army is now but "splendid mercenaries," and the symbolic sceptre of Solomon disappears. The last line of the chapter is a paraphrase of King Saul's lament: ". . . he [Alroy] flew to the couch, and throwing himself upon his knees, and, covering his face with his hands, burst into passionate tears, and exclaimed, 'O! my God, I have deserted thee, and now thou hast deserted me!' " (216). Disraeli meaningfully employs the Saul analogue again as Alroy speaks to the spirit of Jabaster who foretells his pupil's defeat. Even after Alroy learns that Schirene and Honain had plotted Jabaster's death, "he dismissed from his intelligence all cognizance of good and evil; he determined, under all circumstances to cling ever to her; he tore from his mind all memory of the late disclosure" (222). The balance has now been shifted to the side opposite the rabbis' total immersion in speculation.

After Alroy's capture by the Karasmians, Honain (now working for the new conquerors) delivers the terms by which David can save himself and his sister: a public renunciation of the principles which had guided him to his former victories. But Alroy refuses, and thus Disraeli has his protagonist finally accept his commitment once again; in a grand moment, Alroy suffers death rather than complete and public renunciation of the validity of his tradition.[12] So the novel concludes. Although in itself not one of its author's more effective works, in its ideational complexities *Alroy* emerges as significant in terms of Disraeli's later development in the Young England novels, especially in *Tancred*.

V Henrietta Temple (1837) *and* Venetia (1837)

Perhaps the most meaningful comment on *Henrietta Temple* and *Venetia* was made by Disraeli himself when he was writing these novels: "If the results are what my publisher anticipates, and I am able to complete this engagement [ten solid weeks of writing during which *Henrietta Temple* had already been completed and *Venetia* well on its way to completion], I think between £3000 and £4000 might be poured into my coffers by May."[13] The fact of the matter is that in 1836 and 1837 Disraeli was experiencing the most severe financial pressures of his life, and he was attempting to achieve economic solvency through the sales of these two novels. And this economic factor best explains the change of literary pace reflected in *Henrietta Temple* and *Venetia*.

These two novels occupy an anomalous position in any thematic study of Disraeli's novels. They are the only works between *Alroy* and *Coningsby*, but they bear no relationship either to those novels which preceded them or to the Young England novels which followed. Few of the motifs and ideas which are developed fully in the novels of the 1840's and presented in various tentative forms in the earlier novels appear in either *Henrietta Temple* or *Venetia*. Furthermore, both of these works appear in the years immediately following the *Vindication of the English Constitution,* but neither deals with the concerns so forcefully articulated in that work. Once again, the answer must be found in Disraeli's need for money and in his desire to write what he considered popular, saleable fiction. Thus the thematic distance between these two works and those which preceded and those which followed is understandable, although disappointing.

Henrietta Temple has the factitious interest of being a love story written by a novelist in love with a woman whose name was, indeed, Henrietta. Small reason, we might suggest, for a novel to be remembered; and *Henrietta Temple* is not a memorable novel. However, it was not without a popular interest; and it does have its better moments, albeit not enough of them to give the novel a life independent of its relation to Disraeli. The only motif of the earlier novels carried on in this work is Disraeli's interest in Roman Catholicism. The Armine family is Catholic; and their friend and adviser, Glastonbury, is a medieval and Catholic scholar who exerts some salutary influences. The world of politics plays but a small role, taking a central position for only a moment during the last paragraphs of the book.

On the other hand, although of no ideational concern, the love affair between Ferdinand and Henrietta is well managed by Disraeli as he continues to improve as a craftsman. The pacing of the story and its reasonably tight structure foreshadow at least these characteristics of the trilogy. His description of the spunging house is excellent, and his eye for the ludicrous and the pretentious remains sharp. In the final analysis, however, the novel is neither typical nor meaningful in Disraeli's canon; for it carries within it few ideas or authorial observations, and Disraeli's fundamental interests for us are as a novelist of ideas and as a writer of personal involvement and observation. In *Henrietta Temple* and *Venetia,* Disraeli stands at some distance from his creations and produces two relatively impersonal works. His effectiveness for us is thereby lessened.

Venetia's primary interest lies in Disraeli's imaginative rendering of Byron and Shelley. Although some striking liberties are taken with biography and chronology (Shelley, for example, is a volunteer general with the American colonists of the Revolutionary War), this novel in its own rights is more interesting than its predecessor and also in terms of two previous motifs: youthful ambition and the amelioration of society. Cadurcis (Byron), who is devoted to the conception of his own image of greatness, is motivated by a burning ambition. In this sense, he is not unlike Vivian Grey, Contarini Fleming, and Alroy. Cadurcis is, however, a distinguished poet; and the same tension we have already seen in Contarini Fleming is present in Lord Cadurcis: "What I shall do I know not; but this I know, the world shall ring with my name; I will be a man, and a great man!" (210). Although his literary success is great, his desire for fame increases: "He was habituated to triumph; it had been his lot to come, to see, and to conquer; even the procrastination of certain success was intolerable to him; his energetic volition could not endure a check" (278). Through his association with Marmion Herbert (Shelley), Cadurcis is exposed to the fusion of the desire for fame and literary talents, a combination much like that which Contarini had experienced at the conclusion of his novel. Cadurcis hears Herbert argue for the poet as a man with a double allegiance: to art and to the amelioration of society.[14] Indeed, Disraeli has him suggest that "poets are the unacknowledged legislators of the world" (459).

We must assume that Cadurcis would have fallen under the spell of Herbert's argument, just as he had come to adore the elder poet as a man. Cadurcis is, we are often told, much like a young Herbert. Furthermore, Cadurcis' ironic rejoinders to Herbert's lectures on the possibilities of regenerating society spring more from his own recent mistreatment by society than from any ideological position in opposition to Herbert's:[15]

"You are welcome to all I have ever written," said Herbert. "Mine were but crude dreams. I wished to see man noble and happy; but if he will persist in being vile and miserable, I must even be content. I can struggle for him no more."

"Well, you opened my mind," said Cadurcis. "I owe you everything; but I quite agree with you that nothing is worth an effort. As for philosophy and freedom, and all that, they tell devilish well in a stanza; but men have always been fools and slaves, and fools and slaves they always will be."

"Nay," said Herbert, "I will not believe that. I will not give up a jot of my conviction of a great and glorious future for human destinies; but its consummation will not be so rapid as I once thought, and in the meantime I die." (434-35)

However, because of the deaths of the two poets in a boating accident, the logical resolution of Cadurcis' tension is not brought to pass. Yet the logic of the novel and of previous ones implies that Cadurcis would finally have come to share Herbert's position. And, regardless of what Herbert says of the tempering of his own ideals, we remember that his favorite literary character remains Don Quixote. Thus Herbert's commitment to the amelioration of society has matured rather than been compromised. I imagine that the later Disraéli might well have sympathized with Marmion Herbert more than with most of his other creations.

CHAPTER 3

Society and Politics:
Coningsby *and* Sybil

T HE 1830's and 1840's witnessed increasing controversy over
the broad question of the "condition of England." Economic,
political, and social questions were being discussed throughout
the island. Landed aristocrats, factory owners, and laborers all
had vested interests at stake; and each group had certain more
or less powerful organizations which acted in its behalf. These
pressure groups lobbied at all levels of government and in all
parts of England in the attempt to sway both parliamentary
legislation and public opinion, and the multi-faceted "condition
of England" question was not allowed to grow dim in the nation's
eye. Corn Law agitation, Chartism, Factory Acts, Poor Laws,
and the Irish question were but several of these facets. Sides were
taken and just as easily and quickly changed. To be sure, the
Whigs overtly opposed the Tories; but often party differences
were blurred. In 1841, for example, Disraeli referred to the new
Tory government under Sir Robert Peel as "Tory men and Whig
measures."

The Reform Bill of 1832 at least acknowledged the rising power
of the "middle-class";[1] and, although that class did not become
politically significant in practical terms for some time, we can
nevertheless perceive an alignment of classes into opposing camps
which added to the muddled view of English politics and social
theory during the 1830's. Also in this area of political reform
there were numerous political and social alignments and realign-
ments. What the members of Young England thought they saw
in these difficult times was compromise and expediency. They
maintained that neither the Tories nor the Whigs believed in
principles which guided their political conduct; in fact, they

doubted that either party had principles in which to believe. In Disraeli's imaginative recording of the Young England movement, its members are often spokesmen for programs of action which, at least in theory, were averse to compromise and which looked above and beyond the expediencies of the moment. We must pause to take notice of the tension between the historical facts of the political and social situation and the often imaginative rendering of them in Disraeli's novels or in the frequently naïve, unrealistic enunciation of them by the actual as well as the fictional men of the Young England group. Although Disraeli was clearly aware of the obviously significant differences between theoretical and practical politics, he had his fictional protagonists constantly ask whether any practical political measures could be considered truly meaningful if they were not superstructured by a commitment to political ideology. Certainly for this reason alone, the Young England movement is significant. For we can see in this group's views of life and conduct certain values that were accepted as good and desirable in themselves; and these values are the bases of the politics of the adherents of Young England. Furthermore, the novels of Disraeli present to us a fictionalized, imaginative statement of these views. Realizing that Disraeli the novelist is but an extension of Disraeli the practicing politician, we can readily appreciate the view of politics in the novels. In essence, we can perceive, therefore, the theoretical political position of Disraeli and his Young England in the novels of the trilogy.

In the General Preface to the collected edition of his novels (1870), Disraeli discusses his intentions in the Young England trilogy. Although much had happened to Disraeli's political ideas since the 1840's,[2] this preface still remains a responsible source for the motivations and ideas of the trilogy. He says that the three novels deal with the same general subject: "the origin and character of our political parties, their influence on the condition of the people of this country, some picture of the moral and physical condition of that people and some intimation of the means by which it might be elevated and improved. . . ."[3] In more precise terms, Disraeli announces his three major themes as "the derivation and character of political parties; the condition of the people which had been the consequence of them; the duties of the Church as a main remedial agency in our present state. . . ."⁴ Although these three themes are interwoven into each book of the trilogy, the essential focus of each volume is on one of them: *Coningsby* deals primarily with the "derivation and character of political parties"; *Sybil*, with "the condition of the people"; and *Tancred*, with the "remedial" role of the Church.

I The Young England Position

When *Coningsby* was published in 1844, Disraeli was still a relative newcomer in Parliament. (He had been first elected an MP for Maidstone only seven years before, in 1837.) To many, the brilliant Disraeli seemed nothing more than a dandy; to others, he was a visionary, a wild-eyed dreamer; to some, he was an outsider trying to break into the circle of the select, and he was therefore scorned; but, to a few young men, Disraeli embodied the noblest political principles and was the "master." The young members of Parliament who gathered around Disraeli saw in him the apostle of a political philosophy congenial to their sensibilities and beneficial to the nation.

The crucial elements of the New Toryism as envisaged by Disraeli are remarkably simple. At the center is Disraeli's proposition that the inspiration for the New Toryism is to be found in the past, not in political abstractions and theorizing in an *a priori* manner. Speaking of his political tenets, Disraeli states that they were arrived at by "the use of ancient forms and the restoration of the past [rather] than by political revolutions founded on abstract ideas."⁵ Furthermore, Disraeli was convinced that the country's future progress was to come about only by a "reconstructed Tory party."

In the view of Young England, the Tory party had lain dormant for sixty years. Although the historical facts indicate that there had been several different governments which often differed in intention and tone, the old Toryism was viewed as complacent and sated by easy, carefree living. Thus, viewing the Tory governments from 1783 to 1830 as essentially of the same cloth, Young England concluded that the reins of government had been in the hands of tradition-bound reactionaries who had faced no threatening political challenge or change. These leaders of the old Toryism were more interested in maintaining the *status quo* than in developing their party's point of view according to the gospel of Young England. Thus Toryism, rather than working as a dynamic, vibrant force in English life, was in the throes of a nearly fatal illness during these critical years.

As the novels often insist, a once meaningful and exceedingly complex political and social philosophy had been allowed to degenerate into a mass of conservative prejudices. Either there would be change or the Tory party would be buried by its more vigorous opponents; as the party stood, young statesmen who were fresh, bright, and enthusiastic could not be attracted to it. Although this view obviously dismisses Tories like George Canning, William Huskisson, and Peel, and although it contradicts the generally held historical reasons for joining political parties (vested interests, family, geographical responsibilities, etc.), the men of Young England strove to invoke ideological principles as the rationale for party affiliation. They insisted, therefore, that beneath the permutations brought about by the reactionaries, the heart of Toryism still beat. A new body, however, was needed; and Disraeli and his Young England adopted the task of re-creating that body, of designing the new clothes.

The Young England position was that traditional Toryism had allowed its original belief in a dynamic concept of society to die because of neglect. Disraeli and Young England were to attempt to revitalize the conception of the state as an organic unity. C. F. Harrold has commented that Disraeli's "conception of the nation was organic, rather than contractual, and thus was an enemy of all liberal doctrine . . . His Toryism was typical in its approach to reform on its social side rather than on its political side; here he was naturally the enemy of the Whigs and Liberals, who, with the Benthamites, placed their trust in political measures."[6] Disraeli announced in the General Preface that "a generous aristocracy round a real throne" must once more be brought about to replace the oligarchy which controlled England. Young England was to educate not only the Tory party but all of England. Englishmen were to be led to realize that the relationship between men was not a contractual one but one based upon loyalties and ideals—an organic rather than a mechanical relationship.

That society was hierarchical was, of course, without question. The "new" aristocracy was to be fully aware of its duty and obligation to its "inferiors." The aristocracy—in good Burkean terms —was to comprehend this duty and to act on the basis of all that represented *noblesse oblige.* Indeed, in this view of societal organization, the aristocracy emerges as an entire social class incorporating the qualities of Carlyle's hero. The Romantics' creative reading of the Kantian distinction between the worlds of noumena and phenomena is here applied to socio-political areas as the aristocracy assumes the "heroic" power to pierce into the world of noumena. Carlyle's distinction between Abbot Hugo and Abbot Samson in *Past and Present* is essentially Young England's distinction between the old Toryism and the new Toryism.

It was during the Parliament of 1841 that several young legislators who had been educated together at Eton and Cambridge attached themselves to Disraeli. Although never a political party in the formal sense, these enthusiastic young men became Disraeli's coterie. George Smythe (the model for the hero of *Coningsby*), Lord John Manners (Lord Henry Sydney in *Coningsby* and *Tancred*), and Alexander Baillie Cochrane (Buckhurst in *Coningsby*) led the group, which became known as Young England. They protested against an age devoid of beauty, emotion, and imagination; and they distrusted an age obsessed with ugliness, reason, and utility. They longed for the medieval past in which they perceived a monarchy which was a principle rather than a mere instrument, a Church which was a spiritual shepherd to its flock, and an aristocracy which was infused with the best aspects of the feudal relationship. In the words of one of Manners' poems:

> Oh would some noble choose again to raise
> The feudal banner of forgotten days
> And live, despising slander's harmless hate,
> The potent ruler of his petty state.
> Then would the different classes once again
> Feel the kind pressure of the social chain.

Thus Young England was committed to restoring the throne to a position of dignity and real influence; the Church to its former and true position of spiritual and, indeed, secular leadership; and the aristocracy to a position by which it would elevate the lower social orders, thus releasing them from their bonds of misery. At the heart of these beliefs lay a re-awakened belief in idealism and an antipathy toward emerging middle-class values. Young England was concerned with individual man's moral state and physical well-being rather than with his political or economic freedoms. The ideas of Coleridge, Burke, and Carlyle permeated the group. Society, a dynamic, spiritual organism, was not an amoral mechanical jungle in which man's only duty to his fellow man was based on cash payment. Fundamentally, these earnest young men had an abiding faith in their reading of the philosophy of Toryism.

II Coningsby, Sybil, and Young England

In *Coningsby* we are introduced to the epitome of the Young England movement. Harry Coningsby sounds the battle cry when he announces his view of the Tory party to his grandfather:

"But what are they organized for?" said Coningsby. "At best to turn out the Whigs. And when you have turned out the Whigs, what then? You may get your ducal coronet, sir. But a duke now is not as great a man as a baron was but a century back. We cannot struggle against the irresistible stream of circumstances. Power has left our order; this is not an age for factitious aristocracy. As for my grandmother's barony, I should look upon the termination of its abeyance in my favor as the act of my political extinction. What we want, sir, is not to fashion new dukes and furbish up old baronies, but to establish great principles which may maintain the realm and secure the happiness of the people. Let me see authority once more honoured; a solemn reverence again the habit of our lives; let me see property acknowledging as in the old days of faith, that labour is his twin brother, and that the essence of all tenure is the performance of duty; let results such as these be brought about, and let me participate, however feebly, in the great fulfilment; and public life then indeed becomes a noble career, and a seat in parliament an enviable distinction." (434)

In both *Coningsby* and *Sybil*, Disraeli introduces a young, graceful, and brilliant aristocrat as the hero: Harry Coningsby, in the former; Charles Egremont, in the latter. In each case, the hero has assumed the "naturalness" of English life and the correctness of the English social structure. He has been born to and nurtured by the upper class, and his field of vision is naturally delimited by his class. But, in each novel, the young noble is so circumstanced by the author that he becomes aware of English life beyond his class's field of vision; and through this awareness he matures politically, morally, and socially. Kathleen Tillotson has remarked that "one thing the heroes of these novels [the Young England trilogy] have in common: . . . all *think*—perhaps ineffectively, ignorantly, fitfully, but in their puzzled or impulsive way they do think, and about their social rights and responsibilities."[7] As developed by Disraeli, the heroes' speculations and experiences can lead them to only one logical conclusion: the efficacy of the goals of Young England. Both novels are, in their broadest scope, highly symbolic. In each we have an emblematic marriage: Coningsby marries Edith Millbank, and Egremont is united with Sybil Gerard. These unions represent the joining of aristocracy with trade, and the combining of the Tories with the people.[8] Within the framework of these unions which are discussed later, we can perhaps better understand the direction and movement of the novels.

Although the particular focus of *Coningsby* is on the political area of life and although the particular focus of *Sybil* is on the social, both novels combine to present a clear view of Disraeli's conception of meaningful, traditional political principles. Disraeli presents in *Coningsby* a sweeping, panoramic view of the political scene in England from the passing of the Reform Bill in 1832 to the Tory victory in 1841. Against this backdrop, the story of Coningsby himself is developed. When we first meet him at Eton, he is a mere boy unknown by society and knowing little of it. In terms of the values of his class, he is a most fortunate young man; for his grandfather, the wealthy and powerful Lord Monmouth, has taken a special interest in him. It is early in the novel that Harry is first presented to his grandfather. (We can indeed trace the growth of Coningsby by viewing only the several meetings which take place between grandfather and grandson.)

Lord Monmouth epitomizes the forces which Young England

believes are in control of the Tory party. He is wealthy and fully aware of the tremendous power at his disposal. The primary object of his party must be to hold tenaciously to the *status quo;* no more ground must be lost to the "levellers." For his fellow human beings, the Lord feels little more than contempt; but, since he admires wealth, he has some respect for the exceedingly wealthy. A voluptuary, he gathers around him those who can either please his sensual appetites or perform his more trying and routine duties. Lord Monmouth is, therefore, the logical product of what Young England would label perverted, moribund Toryism; his "contempt for mankind was absolute; not a fluctuating sentiment, not a mournful conviction ebbing and flowing with circumstances, but a fixed, profound, unalterable instinct" (190). Political action for Lord Monmouth is no more than a means for achieving an object; in the terms of his Toryism, that object could be nothing other than increased personal power and prestige. Monmouth says to Harry: "After all, what is the end of all parties and all politics? To gain your object. I want to turn our coronet into a ducal one, and to get your grandmother's barony called out of abeyance in your favour" (432).

In *Sybil,* which covers the years from 1837 to 1844, Disraeli satirizes this purely personal desire on the part of the aristocracy. The Egremont family, which prides itself on its noble lineage, had sprung from a domestic servant to one of the favorites of King Henry VIII: "But the house of Marney had risen to high rank; counted themselves ancient nobility; and turned up their noses at the Pratts and Smiths, the Jenkinsons and the Robinsons of our degenerate days; and never had done anything for the nation or for their honours. And why should they now? It was unreasonable to expect it" (14). It is from this background that Charles Egremont comes. So it is that both aristocrats, Egremont and Coningsby, begin at identical starting points and, moved by various, carefully constructed motivating influences, come to awareness of the condition of England and of the goals of Young England.

Disraeli continues his attack on the state of the Conservative party in his satirical portrait of Sir Vavasour Firebrace and his great plans for the baronets. Vavasour, concerned only with the resurrection of the baronetcy to its former position of honor and glory, has the slogan, "once a baronet, always a baronet" (*Sybil,* 121); and he yearns for the restoration of noble costumes and processions. He leads a small group which has petitioned the government, and he confides in the still unaware Egremont: "I am prepared myself, great as would be the sacrifice, even to renounce the claim of the secondary titles for our eldest sons, if, for instance, they would secure us our coronet" (*Sybil,* 60).

Is it any wonder, therefore, that both Coningsby and Egremont begin to question their party? Coningsby asks what the Conservatives aim to conserve. What can the Tories have as goals when the Monmouths and Egremonts desire only personal advancement and care not for the duties of rank; when the Tadpoles' and Tapers' definition of political science is common coin: "To receive £1200 per annum is government; to try to receive £1200 per annum is opposition; to wish to receive £1200 per annum is ambition" (*Coningsby,* 275); when Lady St. Julians, a shrewd observer of the political scene, announces that an invitation to a dinner buys an MP's vote; when a noble boy's idea of a manly career centers upon rotten boroughs and getting something for doing nothing (*Sybil,* 34); when the power of the sovereign has become a mere superstition; when the Church has been desecrated and plundered; when the working classes are in a state of great suffering; and when nobles can still say "If we nobles do not make a stand against the levelling spirit of the age, I am at a loss to know who will fight the battle" (*Sybil,* 118), and "In my opinion, this [fires set by angry laborers] is a mere anti-corn-law riot to frighten the Government; and suppose they do stop the mills—what then? I wish they were all stopped, and then one might live like a gentleman again" (*Sybil,* 406)?

After a Conservative political victory, Coningsby and his friends summarize the state of the Conservative party and the Conservative cause:

"By Jove," said the panting Buckhurst, throwing himself on the sofa, "it was well done: never was anything better done. An immense triumph! The greatest triumph the Conservative cause has had. And yet!" he added, laughing, "if any fellow were to ask me what the Conservative cause were, I am sure I should not know what to say."

"Why it's the cause of our glorious institutions," said Coningsby. "A crown robbed of its prerogatives; a church controlled by a commission; and an aristocracy that does not lead."

"Under whose genial influence, the order of the peasantry, 'a country's pride,' has vanished from the face of the land," said Henry Sydney, "and is succeeded by a race of serfs, who are called labourers and who burn ricks."

"Under which," continued Coningsby, "the crown has become a cipher; the church a sect; the nobility drones; and the people drudges."

"It is the great constitutional cause," said Lord Vere, "that refuses everything to opposition; yields everything to agitation; conservative in parliament, destructive out of doors; that has no objection to any change provided only it be effected by unauthorised means."

"The first public association of men," said Coningsby, "who have worked for an avowed end, without enunciating a single principle."

"And who have established political infidelity throughout the land," said Lord Henry. (*Coningsby*, 277-78)

On the subject of principles, Coningsby fires his companions, for he asks that they rise above parties "and discover some great principles to guide us, to which we may adhere, and which then, if true, will ultimately guide and control others" (279). Moreover, the remedial agency for ailing England must be principles.

In answer to Lord Monmouth's pronouncements of his political beliefs, Coningsby answers with the goals which were to form a portion of Young England's credo (see page 66 above). The hierarchical societal fabric of the feudal past in which authority was duly and sincerely honored must once more be brought into existence. The nobility (property) must take upon itself the mantle of duty, of obligation, of *noblesse oblige* to those beneath. The sovereign must again be supreme, just as government must be thought of as divine. The Church, through whose efforts in both the ecclesiastical and secular spheres mankind could be elevated, must be allowed to play again its free and significant role in English life. The individual human being, regardless of which socio-economic class he belongs to, must be led to a position more closely approximating that of the "happy craftsman" of the Middle Ages. A harmonious state of nature, of worldly existence, must once more emerge. Underlying most of these considerations, Young England asserted the need for the *hero* to emerge from the ashes of the present state of English nobility and politics, and, guided by principles, to lead his fellow men.

There is little question that Disraeli was significantly influenced by the Kantian distinction between the realms of phenomena and noumena as interpreted by the Romantics, Burke, and Carlyle. Furthermore, Disraeli also shared the broad corollary concept of the hero as that individual uniquely in tune with the realm of noumena.[9] In each novel of the trilogy—and in *Coningsby* and *Sybil* in the particular sense of the political—Disraeli articulates the Young England conception of the hero. Over and over, the author stresses the need for such a personage and carefully and fully delineates his characteristics.

III *The Hero*

Sidonia sets the tone for a discussion of the heroic motif in Disraeli's works: "Man is made to adore and to obey; but if you will not command him; if you give him nothing to worship; he will fashion his own divinities, and find a chieftain in his own passions" (*Coningsby*, 253). Such a statement echoes the theoretical medieval conceptions of political authority: the natural inequality of men, the divine derivation of temporal authority, and the moral and ethical functions of authority.[10] The hero must be guided by great principles, rise above the mere expediencies of parties, and guide and control others.

Disraeli's hero fits neatly into the heroic mold created by Disraeli's predecessors. Not only can the hero move easily in the world of phenomena and thereby perceive what ails society, but he can also pierce below phenomena into the realm of noumena and seize hold of the methods, the great principles, by which society can be cured. In every sense of the phrase, the hero must be the legislator of mankind. Of the heroic feeling, Disraeli says:

It was that noble ambition, the highest and the best, that must be born in the heart and organised in the brain; which will not let a man be content unless his intellectual power is recognised by his race, and desires that it should contribute to their welfare. It is the heroic feeling; the feeling that in old days produced demi-gods; without which no state is safe; without which political institutions are meat without salt; the crown a bauble, the church an establishment, parliaments debating clubs, and civilisation itself but a fitful and transient dream. (*Coningsby*, 274)

Such a hero is obviously incapable of functioning within a framework of democratic society; the hierarchical societal fabric is this hero's element. Society must, therefore, be re-structured in medieval terms; and, in Sidonia's words, the essential nature of man demands such a closely structured society. To better understand this crucially important concept—that of the hero—in Disraeli's invocation of pre-Reformation and feudal England, a sketch of the hero and the ramifications of the heroic as presented by Disraeli is necessary.

Throughout the Young England trilogy, Disraeli constantly reinforces the genius and the divine destiny of the hero. Since man was made to adore and obey, and since he has to be commanded in order to have his lot in life elevated, the nature of the leader or commander is of cardinal importance. The efficacy of the hero would be in direct proportion to his genius and divinely inspired insights. The Disraelian hero thus becomes a combination of medieval law-giver and Carlylean hero. Disraeli announces that "A cause is a great abstraction, and fit only for students; embodied in a party, it stirs men to action; but place at the head of that party a leader who can inspire enthusiasm, he commands the world. Divine faculty!" (*Coningsby*, 112). The leader to Disraeli has "a finer temperament susceptible of receiving the impressions and imbibing the inspirations of superior, yet sympathising spirits" (*Coningsby*, 114-15). The hero is "a primordial and creative mind; one that will say to his fellows, 'Behold, God has given me thought; I have discovered truth, and you shall believe!'" (*Coningsby*, 115).

In both *Coningsby* and *Sybil*, Disraeli presents young aristocrats in the process of becoming educated in the school of the heroic. Both Coningsby and Egremont not only come to understand the functions of the hero within the framework of Young England, but they also come to realize their own "heroism." Egremont, for example, learns that he is inevitable; and through the teachings of Sidonia and through his relationships with his peers, Harry Coningsby gradually becomes aware of himself as a hero. At Eton it had been Coningsby around whom the intellectual, romantically oriented young men gathered. Edith Mill-bank says to Harry: "you have such a band of friends, Oswald was saying this morning there was no one who had so many devoted friends" (*Coningsby*, 391-92). Coningsby answers that they are all united by sympathy in common principles, and he adds that sympathy is the only true bond of friendship. At this stage in his development, however, the young man has not yet attempted any analysis of his situation. Nevertheless, shortly after the above exchange, "Coningsby felt . . . a profound conviction which never again deserted him, that the conduct which violates the affections of the heart or the dictates of the conscience, however it may lead to immediate success, is a fatal error" (439).

In order to revitalize and rejuvenate the conservative cause, the *true* Toryism, Coningsby must disengage himself from the morally strangling and intellectually stultifying two-party system. In the process of rising above the Whigs and the Tories, Coningsby looks back to Bolingbroke, Henry St. John: "Assuredly the genius of Bolingbroke . . . would have . . . recoiled from such men and such measures on the contemporary political scene" (*Coningsby*, 74). Disraeli lauds Bolingbroke: "The fine genius of the injured Bolingbroke, the only peer of his period who was educated, and proscribed by the oligarchy because they were afraid of his eloquence, 'the glory of his order and the shame,' shut out from Parliament, found vent in those writings which recalled to the English people the inherent blessings of their old free monarchy, and painted in the immortal hues his picture of the patriot king . . ." (*Sybil*, 18). Coningsby thus adopts the patriot king motif and rises above the concept of party. The individual man, touched by greatness, genius, and perhaps even by divinity, guided by great principles, must rule; and this indeed was the secret of all wisdom taught him by Sidonia.

Thinking of the teeming millions of London, Coningsby muses:

But a word from his lip, a thought from his brain expressed at the right time, at the right place, might turn their hearts, might influence their passions, might change their opinions, might affect their destiny. Nothing is great but the personal. As civilisation advances, the accidents of life become each day less important. The power of man, his greatness and his glory, depend on essential qualities. Brains every day become more precious than blood. You must give men new ideas, you must teach them new words, you must modify their manners, you must change their laws, you must root out prejudices, subvert convictions, if you wish to be great. (*Coningsby*, 480)

Indeed, the language used by Disraeli in describing the triumphant return of Coningsby to Darlford, which had elected him to Parliament, reinforces the fact that Coningsby has not only learned what a hero must be but has himself become one. He is received "as if he were a prophet" (*Coningsby*, 499), and "There were a great many present at that moment who though they had never seen Coningsby 'before, would willingly have then died for him. Coningsby had touched their hearts, for he had spoken from his own. His spirit had entirely magnetized them. Darlford believed in Coningsby; and a very good creed" (501).

IV *The Growth of Coningsby and Egremont*

The development of Coningsby, from an unaware young aristocrat through his conflict with his environment and family tradition and finally to the status of the heroic, is easily traced. However, the character of Sidonia and his influence on Coningsby's growth have often been confusing problems in the past. If we view Sidonia as a dynamic, real "flesh and blood" character in the novel, we reach an impasse. Sidonia does not develop; he is, if anything, a flat, static character. His speeches often read like the grossest, most insensitive intrusions on the part of the author. His meetings with Coningsby are contrived and patently coincidental. As a man, Sidonia is sexless, emotionless, and, in a word, sub-human. To consider him a developed character is impossible. Whatever other defects Disraeli has as a novelist, such an obvious lack of skill in depicting the human animal is not one of them. Indeed, Disraeli is rather successful in character portrayal. Often, as in the cases of Lord Monmouth and Baptist Hatton, for example, he can incisively create a character while practicing the greatest word economy.

To find the true role of Sidonia, we must look at him as something other than a bona fide character. In reality he is ambivalent. On the one hand, Sidonia has the role of a chorus through which Disraeli renders his own views, as well as society's, on subjects only tangentially related to the novel. More importantly, on the other hand, Sidonia is the very incarnation of the hero—the heroic conscience. Therefore, that he comes to instruct Coningsby at crucial points is not coincidental, just as we do not label as coincidental Athene's coming to Odysseus or indeed Christmas Past to Scrooge. Sidonia might very well be emblematic of the spiritual or divine guidance by which the hero is aided. Disraeli makes perfectly clear Sidonia's superhuman abilities: he knows everything, speaks all tongues, advises all heads of states, is superior to all men in wealth and worldly understanding, can claim no country for his own, but is honored and welcomed in all countries. In short, Sidonia is not a "character" in the normal sense; he is a device by which Disraeli leads Coningsby to a realization of the heroic.

In *Sybil*, Egremont undergoes a growth of awareness which parallels Coningsby's. If Egremont's progress appears to be different, it does so only because of the development of the subject matter in *Sybil*: Egremont is more closely concerned with practical political problems than was Coningsby. Where Disraeli introduced us to the origins and principles of the Young England movement in *Coningsby,* he presents it in practical action in *Sybil*. Fundamentally, Egremont's pilgrimage is Coningsby's: from a young, unaware aristocrat to an apostle of the *new* Toryism. The start of Egremont's rebirth, however, is highly dramatic and emotional in contrast to Coningsby's gradual and intellectual movement toward realization.

While on a walk through the countryside, Egremont comes upon the ruins of a great abbey. It is dusk as he stops to ponder the remains: "never without emotion could he behold these unrivalled remains of one of the greatest religious houses of the North" (*Sybil*, 66). With the setting sun throwing the scene into shadows at the end of a warm, glorious day, the stage is set for a pregnant moment:

But it was in the centre of this tract of ruins, occupying a space of not less than two acres, that, *with a strength which had defied time, and with a beauty which had at last turned away the wrath of man,* still rose, if not in perfect, yet admirable form and state, one of the noblest achievements of Christian art—the abbey church. The summer vault was now its only roof, and all that remained of its gorgeous windows was the vastness of their arched symmetry, and some wreathed relics of their fantastic frame-work, but the rest was un-injured. (67 [italics mine])

At this place—a powerful link with the feudal past—and in his reflective frame of mind, doubly stirred by the juxtaposition of the time of day and the physical surroundings, Egremont is in a perfect psychological position to receive Sybil, Walter Gerard, and Stephen Morley. Just as Sidonia (the spirit of the new and medievally oriented Toryism) had been Coningsby's teacher, so Sybil and Gerard become the means through which Egremont comes to accept the new Toryism. Charles is told that "with the monasteries expired the only hope [of community] that we ever had in England. . . . There is no community in England; there is aggregation, but aggregation under circumstances which make it rather a dissociating than a uniting principle" (75). Egremont is stunned by the revelations wrought by Gerard, especially by the realization that there are indeed in England two nations: the rich and the poor. Reinforcing the beginning of rebirth in Charles Egremont, Disraeli concludes the scene:

At this moment a sudden flush of rosy light, suffusing the gray ruins, indicated that the sun had just fallen; and, through a vacant arch that overlooked them, alone in the resplendent sky, glittered the twilight star. The hour, the scene, the solemn stillness and the soften-ing beauty, repressed controversy, induced even silence. The last words of the stranger lingered in the ear of Egremont; his musing spirit was teeming with many thoughts, many emotions; when from the Lady's chapel there rose the evening hymn to the Virgin. A single voice; but tones of almost supernatural sweetness; tender and solemn, yet flexible and thrilling. (77)

The voice of Sybil announces the setting of the sun, the end of another day, and the irrevocable end of one phase of Charles Egremont's existence.

Thus, just as Coningsby moved from his aristocratic birthright —the Tory *status quo*—to a socio-political position paralleling that of Young England, so Egremont follows a similar pattern. In order to dissociate himself more completely from that birth-right, Egremont takes on an assumed identity, leaves his own *milieu*, and goes among Gerard's people. Not only is Charles in a better position to understand the condition of England, but, by this move, he is better able to learn from Gerard and Sybil. This learning process is not an easy one, although it does develop into a complete one: we see a new Egremont when Charles finally feels it time to enter Parliament. Prior to his meeting with the Gerards, Egremont had vague stirrings of discontentment, as he longed for a goal toward which he might work: "He was now conscious he wanted an object; and was ever musing over action, though as yet ignorant how to act" (41).

In retrospect, Egremont realized the importance of the meeting at the abbey: "It seemed to Egremont that, from the day he met these persons at the Abbey ruins, the horizon of his experience had insensibly expanded; more than that, there were streaks of light breaking in the distance, which already gave a new aspect to much that was known, and which perhaps was ultimately destined to reveal much that was now utterly obscure" (154). But not until he had completed his apprenticeship and was actively engaged in practical politics did Egremont fully realize what he had learned:

In a parliamentary sense, that great party [the true Toryism] has ceased to exist; but I will believe that it still lives in the thought and sentiment and consecrated memory of the English nation. It has its origin in great principles and in noble instincts; it sympathizes with the lowly, it looks up to the Most High; it can count its heroes and its martyrs; they have met in its behalf plunder, proscription, and death. Nor, when it finally yielded to the iron progress of oligarchical supremacy, was its catastrophe inglorious. Its genius was vindicated in golden sentences and with fervent arguments of impassioned logic by St. John; and breathed in the intrepid eloquence and patriot soul of William Wyndham. Even now it is not dead, but sleepeth; and, in an age of political materialism, of confused purposes and perplexed intelligence, that aspires only to wealth because it has faith in no other accomplishment, as men rifle cargoes on the verge of shipwreck, Toryism will yet rise from the tomb over which Bolingbroke shed his last tear, to bring back strength to the Crown, liberty to the subject, and to announce that power has only one duty—to secure the social welfare of the PEOPLE. (317-18)

Egremont also came to accept two cardinal facts: the natural supremacy of some men over others (of Gerard over others for example), and the unquestionable truth of England's division into "two nations." A commonplace of medieval political thought maintains that all men are equal only in the sight of God; and, as Coningsby learned, that is the only true basis of equality. The following assessment of the medieval political situation compares with what Egremont has stated above: "In politics, they [the medieval thinkers] thought the function of the state is moral, that law and its administration should be imbued with Christian ideas of justice, and that the relations of ruler and ruled should always be founded on reciprocal obligation. The state, property, and the family are all trusts from God to those who control them, and they must be used to further divine purposes. Finally, the medieval ideal included the strong belief that all nations and peoples are part of one great community."[11]

Thus, after having been thoroughly indoctrinated into the ways of the new Toryism, Egremont carries on from precisely that point at which *Coningsby* concludes. At the conclusion of the first novel of the trilogy, Coningsby had just been elected to Parliament. He would now have a practical and real opportunity to put into operation the many theories which heretofore had been treated in an intellectual vacuum, and Disraeli brings the novel to its close by asking a series of questions:

They [the men of Young England] stand now on the threshold of public life. They are in the leash, but in a moment they will be slipped. What will be their fate? Will they maintain in august assemblies and high places the great truths which in study and in solitude they have embraced? Or will their courage exhaust itself in the struggle, their enthusiasm evaporate before hollow-hearted ridicule, their generous impulses yield with a vulgar catastrophe to the tawdry temptations of a low ambition? Will their skilled intelligence subside into being the adroit tool of a corrupt party? Will vanity confound their fortunes, or jealousy wither their sympathies? Or will they remain brave, single, and true; refuse to bow before shadows and worship phrases; sensible of the greatness of their position, recognise the greatness of their duties; denounce to a perplexed and disheartened world the frigid theories of a generalising age that have destroyed the individuality of man; and restore the happiness of their country by believing in their own energies, and daring to be great? (502-03)

In *Sybil* we discover the answers to many of these questions.

Egremont becomes an MP cast upon the mold of Disraeli him-self—or, at least, upon an idealized mold of Disraeli as the author would have liked to have been able to view himself. Having profited by his experiences with Gerard and his half of the English nation, Egremont boldly launches into a course of action in support of that "second nation." Not afraid to incur the dis-pleasure and indeed ridicule of his fellows, he constantly lends his support to "unpopular" causes. For example, in regard to the Chartist Petition of 1839, Egremont's devotion to what he had learned at Mowbray motivates his inspired speech in behalf of the Petition (a speech, as a matter of fact, which was not unlike Disraeli's under similar circumstances). There is, of course, much more in the novel: great scenes of Chartist agitation, the incredible town of Wodgate, Gerard's final victories, and the marriage of Egremont to Sybil. However, the consideration at hand is the change wrought in Egremont. It is worth adding that just as Coningsby had his Sidonia, so Egremont had his Sybil. Although Sybil is a more highly developed character than Sidonia, she is by no means a dynamic one; in fact, her speeches often read like Sidonia's.

V *The Two Nations and the Responsibility of the Aristocracy*

Politics and government must rise above the unreal and un-fortunate concept of parties to become concerned with divine ends. In his General Preface, Disraeli announces that "the feudal system may have worn out, but its main principle—that the tenure of property should be the fulfillment of duty—is the essence of good government. The divine right of kings may have been a plea for feeble tyrants, but the divine right of govern-ment is the keystone of human progress. . . ."[12] The influence of Burke's theory of Natural Law is clearly in evidence here, just as we see in this declaration its debt to the political structure of the Middle Ages. Disraeli's biographer, W. F. Monypenny, states: "In a passage such as that, which contains the kernal of Disraeli's teaching, we feel the sentiment that gives to Toryism its power over the imagination; and for lack of which Liberalism, in spite of its self-confident and triumphant advance, remains in comparison mechanical and uninspiring, invested in mediocrity, stamped with the seal of the commonplace, and profoundly unsatisfying to the deeper spirits of every age."[13] To be sure, Monypenny's partisan attitude permeates his estimate; and yet he isolates one of the great motivating factors in the entire Young England movement: the desire to satisfy the deeper spirits of every man. The movement above and beyond political parties is aimed at precisely this goal.

Whenever Young England speaks of principles and political action, one must again recall that tension previously alluded to between the historical facts and the imaginative rendering of them. A convincing argument can be developed around the proposition that British politics of the Victorian years—including the most successful and far reaching political and diplomatic actions—were predicated more on an attempt to cope with the situation of the moment than to apply great principles to the situation of the moment. On the other hand, however, a convincing argument can be developed in support of the thesis that Disraeli more often articulated principles than perhaps any other nineteenth-century Conservative leader. Certainly the Conservative leader who is seen most frequently in the trilogy and who is in reality perhaps second only to Disraeli in stature in the history of the Conservative Party in nineteenth-century England, Sir Robert Peel, differed sharply from Disraeli on this matter of principles. R. B. McDowell suggests the following: "Peel . . . was more concerned with preserving and increasing his well merited reputation for political seriousness and administrative competence than elaborating his party's doctrinal position. . . . Unlike Burke or Disraeli he rarely embarked on an exposition of general principles; indeed, early in the first reformed parliament he cautioned the house against wasting its energies on abstract resolutions."[14]

The tension between historical fact and imaginative history is made more taut by Asa Briggs's remark concerning the Peel-Disraeli antagonism: "Disraeli himself had no positive policy and did little in Parliament to justify his pre-occupation as a novelist with the 'condition of England question.'" Briggs adds that Disraeli did not "support an 1842 motion in favour of outdoor relief to the poor, which mustered only twenty-two radical votes; he

Society and Politics

attacked the education grant of 1839; he took no part in the
Mines Act debates; and he voted against the Public Health Act
of 1848."[15] One, of course, could go on. Disraeli's interest in the
1867 Reform Bill was, for example, totally pragmatic and fundamentally in opposition to the Young England credo of twenty
years back. Thus, even though the tension must be ever acknowledged, one must exercise care lest he overlook the ideological
commitments that the practicing politician did indeed share with
his imaginative creations.

Because the hierarchical societal fabric of the feudal past had
its effect upon the Young England movement, it is important
to note how Disraeli develops this fabric in his manifesto. We
have, of course, already seen several intimations of this broad
concept of a structured society in the discussions of the hero, of
guiding principles, and of the divine duties of government.
Furthermore, we know Young England believed that *noblesse
oblige* in its highest sense theoretically permeated the medieval
world. Whether we view medieval society in its ecclesiastical or
in its secular phase, we find that authority was duly and sincerely
honored. Conversely, however, authority was to be always deeply
aware of its duties and obligations to those individuals and
groups on lower social and/or economic levels. Loyalty and faith
were to bind medieval men one to the other and to their institutions be they religious, economic or governmental. The nexus of
society was faith; feudal relations were predicated upon obligations on the parts of both lord and vassal.

The basic premises of such a reciprocal relationship appealed
to Young England, especially in an era which witnessed such
flagrant abuses of authority and power. Sidonia had said that
man was made to adore and obey, but whom could man adore
when England was divided into two nations, when England's
two nations were fragmented into numerous power-mongering
and assiduously selfish groups? Obviously, all sides were at fault;
but Disraeli's group placed the greatest onus of blame on the
Tory aristocrats whose primary goal, according to Young England, was to maintain the *status quo*. Rather than the medieval
reciprocal relationship, nineteenth-century England was faced
with a dire situation in which the poor and the rich failed to

communicate with each other—the rich were unconcerned; the poor had little power. Two colliers in *Sybil* summarize the situation:

"Atween the poor man and the gentleman there never was no connexion, and that's the wital mischief of this country."

"It's a very true word . . . and by this token that when we went to play [went on strike] in '28, and the masters said they would meet us; what did they do but walk around the ground and speak to the butties [the mine owners' middlemen]. The butties had their ear."

"We never want no soldiers here if the masters would speak with the men; but the sight of a pitman is pison to a gentleman, and if we go up to speak with 'em, they always run away." (168)

Thus the aristocracy, the landowners, must once more act upon the obligations inherent in their positions. The precise nature of the aristocracy's obligations or duties falls into three areas: (1) the individual laborer's position must be elevated to a condition paralleling as closely as possible that of the medieval craftsman; (2) the sovereign and the government must be seen as divinely inspired; and (3) the Church within the broad framework of its many secular ramifications must become again a significant force in the life of England and her people. When Coningsby saw for the first time the Millbank factory, Disraeli describes the scene in charged language: "Coningsby beheld in this great factory the last and the most refined inventions of mechanical genius. The building had been fitted up by a capitalist as anxious to raise a monument of the skill and power of his order, as to obtain a return for the great investment" (*Coningsby*, 172). The word *order* is crucial, for in every sense of the word Millbank is a secular monastery. The industrialist's clerk "detailed to Coningsby the plans which Mr. Millbank had pursued both for the moral and physical well-being of his people; how he had built churches, and schools, and institutes; houses and cottages on a new system of ventilation; how he had allotted gardens; established singing classes" (*Coningsby*, 172). The new aristocracy must acknowledge the Millbanks as members, just as it must follow the lead of Millbank and Trafford who have heeded Carlyle's plea that the buccaneers become the captains of industry. The new aristocracy must bear in mind Disraeli's claim that "Power and the People are both divine" (*Sybil*, 44).

What the three areas of aristocratic obligation must lead to is a recognition of the harmonious nature of existence in which the various gears of society mesh smoothly. Furthermore, that harmony of which Disraeli spoke could come to pass only under the leadership of the aristocracy. Egremont, in attempting to convince Sybil that the people cannot lead the coming change in England, points to Disraeli's assumption:

The people are not strong; the people never can be strong. Their attempts at self-vindication will end only in their suffering and confusion. It is civilisation that has effected, that is effecting, this change. It is that increased knowledge of themselves that teaches the educated their social duties. There is a dayspring in the history of this nation, which perhaps those only who are on the mountain-tops can as yet recognise. You deem you are in darkness, and I see a dawn. The new generation of the aristocracy of England are not tyrants, not oppressors. . . . Their intelligence, better than that, their hearts are open to the responsibility of their position. But the work that is before them is no holiday-work. It is not the fever of superficial impulse that can remove the deep-fixed barriers of centuries of ignorance and crime. Enough that their sympathies are awakened; time and thought will bring the rest. They are the natural leaders of the people, Sybil; believe me they are the only ones. (*Sybil*, 321-22)

Mr. Trafford, the industrialist and younger son of a family centuries old, has realized his obligations to his workpeople and has responded to those obligations. Trafford's factory thrives while his people are well cared for—a combination of events which few industrialists and aristocrats thought possible. His people are housed, fed, clothed, and entertained by the paternalistic Trafford. Although their lives are literally in his debt, the people are satisfied and happy; they are the mythical "happy craftsmen" of the Middle Ages in nineteenth-century England. Under this system of benevolent authoritarianism, the people thrive: "In the settlement of Trafford crime was positively unknown, and offences were very slight. There was not a single person in the village of a reprobate character. The men were well-clad; the women had a blooming cheek; drunkenness was unknown; while the moral condition of the softer sex was proportionately elevated" (*Sybil*, 212). These results compare with the following diagnosis of the medieval situation, parallel to Trafford in every point, by a contemporary psychiatrist, Dr. Gregory Zilboorg:

Families were large and parents were able to live their instinctual lives on a fully adult, genital level. They were physiologically as well as psychologically real fathers and mothers. The cult of an affectionate and obedient attitude toward the actual father and his socialized equivalent was universal. All along the line of psychological father-substitutes—from the benevolent authority of the Church through the protective and considerate authority of the master of the guild to that of the real head of the family—there operated the principle of being loved and taught and protected and being grateful and loving and responsive in return for love and protection at the hands of the father. It was an almost ideal psychological constellation of adulthood, from the standpoint of the proper alignment of instinctual drives.[16]

It is probably true that both Disraeli and Zilboorg are dealing in myths—in historically invalid, unreal views of the medieval world; but any myth gains at least partial life when it is wedded to belief. Disraeli's view of progress, spiraling rather than cyclical, is based on the laws of social organization which he assumed were embodied in the medieval world. Obviously, we can appreciate Disraeli's admiration for Trafford; for his very existence attests to the possibility of carrying over certain aspects of medieval life into the social fabric of nineteenth-century England.[17] The new society is to be based upon the medieval concept of society as a spiritual organism ruled by leaders in whom principles were guiding laws; and Coningsby and Egremont, Sidonia, Millbank, and Trafford, each on a different level, were seen by Disraeli as such leaders. In practical Burkean terms, the sovereign and government are elevated to positions of great moral responsibility; for they are to interpret and carry out the dictates of Natural Law. Government, in this sense, is divine. The individual is seen as the object of the desires of government—and as the object of the desires of the aristocracy both new and old.

Edmund Burke had announced in no uncertain terms that the

logic of feudalism and of the medieval socio-political structure was not invalid for contemporary times even if feudalism itself was void and dead. This Burkean view is precisely the one adopted by Disraeli. To be sure, Disraeli's sensibilities were in tune with his view of the Middle Ages, but his medievalism delves far below the merely superficial. The Young England program was to cut away the trappings—satisfying and pleasant as they in themselves are—and look to the social and political (and religious) principles which the group believed sub-structured them. Obviously, what they found was considered by Disraeli, Coningsby, Egremont, and Trafford to be of absolute value and therefore to be as applicable to nineteenth-century England as they had been to medieval England. They felt that any society so structured gave its citizens infinitely greater opportunities to achieve the good life—a life which they felt transcended the Utilitarians' narrow and expedient concept of the Good.

Yet we are by no means done examining Disraeli's sense of the political past; for we have not yet viewed the area of religion, which, far more than an organized system of worshipping God, was in feudal England the unifying and, indeed, controlling factor in man's life. Government and statecraft were guided by religion just as was every other area of human endeavor. This amazing cultural cohesiveness engendered by the Church is commented upon by Herbert J. Muller: "The famed unity of the Middle Ages is not a mere fiction. There was a practically universal agreement on the basic ideas by which men professed to live. Catholicism was not only the one Church but the primary inspiration of art, the main source of education, the accepted basis of all philosophy, science, political theory, and economic theory."[18]

To understand Disraeli's religious medievalism is to understand not only Disraeli's sense of the past generally but is perhaps also to understand much of Disraeli himself. For, by viewing the philosophy which emerges from the treatment of religion in Disraeli's novels, the reader becomes aware of more than the subject of religion however broadly conceived. If we couple Disraeli's religious medievalism as seen most graphically in Lyle (*Coningsby*), St. Lys (*Sybil*), and *Tancred*, with the novelist's view of history, what must emerge is a world view, a *Weltan-schauung*, so broad that hardly an aspect of human life is left unaccounted for.[19] In fact, the political views which we have just examined must be considered an integral aspect of the religious views which we discuss in Chapter 5.

CHAPTER 4

Meaning in History

LORD Acton believed that "from the study of political thought above all things we derive a conviction of the essential continuity of history."[1] This view is also fundamentally Disraeli's, as it is of most conservative thinkers. In the *Vindication of the English Constitution*, which appeared early in his career (published in December, 1835), Disraeli states that in any age the rulers of the nation must, by looking back into the history of man, "discover certain principles of ancestral conduct, which they acknowledge as the causes that these institutions [the contemporary social, political, and religious institutions] have flourished and descended to them; and in their future career, and all changes, reforms, and alterations, that they may deem expedient, they resolve that these principles shall be their guides and their instructors."[2] In this statement we find the kernel of Disraeli's view of history and of the past.

I *Disraeli and the Past*

In each of the three novels in Disraeli's trilogy, the past significantly influences the present. In each novel the protagonist is brought to see the efficacy of the great principles of the past. He begins in utter frustration after learning that no great principles guide present English life; he concludes in a state of great hope after being led to understand the great principles. He is optimistic about the state that English life could reach if those great principles were practiced. In the first two novels, *Coningsby* and *Sybil*, the apostles of Young England theorize about the principles and attempt to put them into operation through political measures; but they are unsuccessful. In *Tancred*, the concluding novel of the Young England trilogy, Disraeli shifts his attention from politics to religion; and in this novel the super-structure for his organic view of history is erected. The pro-tagonists are constantly instructed to look into the past in order to understand the present and to create a better future: "That's the true spring of wisdom: meditate over the past" (*Coningsby*, 358); "it is the past alone that can explain the present" (*Sybil*, 491).

There was an enormous change taking place in the area of historical interpretation. The views of the fixed, Deistic eighteenth century were being supplanted by the idea of a sweep in history, by the idea of "becoming." The theory was, in brief, that there was a movement in history akin to the scientific, evolutionary movement which Darwin was soon to explode on the Victorian horizon. (Indeed, a short time later in the century, Herbert Spencer and others were to exploit the Darwinian evolutionary process in relation to social man.) This idea of "becoming" devel-oped in many historical and philosophical quarters into an opti-mistic trend; the state of man and therefore of his society was becoming better as generation succeeded generation, and the facts of history could be offered as evidence for this view.

We should be aware of the fact that there arose *two* interpre-tations of the "development" view—one optimistic, the other pessimistic. We know of the Coleridgeans' pessimism concerning the state of economic conflict which they saw in contemporary England. This economic and social warfare, however, was seen as necessary in the development of society by Adam Smith and others such as John Millar in *Observations Concerning the Destruction of Ranks in Society* and Adam Ferguson in *An Essay on the History of Civil Society*. Disraeli would certainly be closer to (but without sharing the same degree of pessimism of) the former group. Jeremy Bentham, representing still another view, believed that history disclosed no laws of development and that organic theories of history might well lead to political reaction.

Disraeli's view of history has much in common with that of the Saint-Simonians[3] and the Germano-Coleridgeans.[4] However, in several crucial areas Disraeli moves away from these groups as he develops his unique attitude toward history. Disraeli shares certain rather popular ideas of Auguste Comte and Saint-Simon, especially with regard to the concept of Progress. He agrees with the Frenchmen in reacting against the eighteenth century's views and in seeing a vital, "becoming" motion in history. But, where Disraeli disagrees, the disagreements are significant. His Progress is a type of forward, *spiraling* motion having as its base the laws and principles of the primitive and Hebraeo-Christian Church. Disraeli would deny the theory of a cyclical pattern in history with its ages of construction and revolution; rather, he sees a flow, albeit an often interrupted one, in the events of history. He would, of course, agree with Saint-Simon's view that the development of happiness is the crucial element, but he would define happiness in a manner different from the Saint-Simonians. (Disraeli, for example, rejected the concepts of democracy and equality.) However, the development of Saint-Simon's views by his disciples in the *Producteur*—the idea of alternation between organic and critical epochs—brings us back to Disraeli's disagreement. (Whether Disraeli read the Saint-Simonians directly, we do not know. But certainly he was aware of their views if from no other source than from Carlyle.[5])

Again, in essence, Disraeli would agree with much that the Saint-Simonians had to suggest, and with Carlyle (prior to *Past and Present,* from which point Carlyle moves from the influence of the Saint-Simonians[6]). For Disraeli, the organic and critical pattern may indeed be a true one in terms of the facts of history; but he could not consider it the proper one in theory. Clearly, Disraeli was more philosopher than historian in his reading of historical pattern. Disraeli would agree with Coleridge's estimate of the type of history which dedicates itself to collecting facts and seeking causes and effects without any committed relation to a sense or spirit of the historical process. Coleridge said: "What can be more striking, in illustration of the utter inadequacy of this line of investigation for arriving at the real truth, than the political treatises and constitutional histories which we have in every library? . . . A takes this class of facts; B takes that class: each proves something true, neither proves *the* truth; or anything like *the* truth; that is the whole truth."[7]

As we shall see in *Tancred,* Disraeli believed that the spiritual movement away from the great traditional principles (of the Middle Ages, for instance) was an error; and his answer to the "great Asian mystery" will make my point clear. Like Burke, Disraeli does not desire a return to feudalism. He recognizes that feudalism cannot be superimposed upon the nineteenth century; but, again like Burke, Disraeli sees certain great principles underlying the feudal system, principles which he believes have cogency for all time. Therefore, the view of history which presents itself to Disraeli is not alternating or cyclical, but spiraling. Mankind moves constantly upward, as it were, from the Middle Ages and before; but in order for this movement to be successful, it not only must be based upon the great principles of the past but must be forever refining and reinterpreting those principles for its own time.

We recall that Disraeli had said, "In *Vivian Grey* I have portrayed my active and real ambition; in *Alroy* my ideal ambition."[8] That Disraeli's "active and real ambition" was realized is obvious. Not so clear, however, is his "ideal ambition." Let us return for a brief further look at *Alroy* which has much in common with *Tancred*. Both novels deal with the past and with Judaism, but Disraeli's thinking on these subjects had not yet been crystallized in 1833 in *Alroy*. But in *Tancred* (1847) we see that Disraeli had come to firmly conceived conclusions about both the past and Judaism. But one value of *Alroy* lies in its presentation—however groping and tentative—of a facet of Disraeli's view of history.

The events of the novel take place in the twelfth century. As we have seen, *Alroy* deals with the desire of David Alroy, a descendant of the House of David, to lift Israel to her former position of glory and grandeur. Beginning as a captive of the Mohammedans, Alroy escapes, goes to Jerusalem, leads an army devoted to his cause, and is successful in his holy war. He wins Western Asia for Israel, but Alroy is not content. He now feels that both he and Israel are invincible, and he desires the world for his God; "The Lord of Hosts" *must* have universal dominion. But the world is too much for Alroy, and he is defeated and taken prisoner once more. He is magnificent in death as he refuses freedom and faces execution rather than abandon his faith. In a grand speech, Alroy answers the charges brought against him by the king of his captors, the Karasmians:

King of Karasmé! I stand here accused of many crimes. Now hear
my answers. 'Tis said I am a rebel. My answer is, I am a Prince as
thou art, of a sacred race, and far more ancient. I owe fealty to no
one but to my God. . . . 'Tis well understood in every polity, my
people stand apart from other nations, and ever will, in spite of
suffering. . . . I am true to a deep faith of ancient days, which
even the sacred writings of thy race still reverence. For the arts
magical I practised, and the communion with infernal powers 'tis said
I held, know, King, I raised the standard of my faith by the direct
commandment of my God, the great Creator of the universe. What
need of magic, then? What need of paltering with petty fiends, when
backed by His omnipotence? My magic was His inspiration. Need I
prove why, with such aid, my people crowded round me? The time
will come when from out our ancient seed, a worthier chief will
rise, not to be quelled even by thee, Sire. (*Alroy*, 261-62)

Since Disraeli said that *Alroy* represented his "ideal ambition,"
he must have felt a kinship with David Alroy; but, as Monypenny points out, Disraeli was far too practical to devote his
life to a religious crusade which had little chance of success.[9]
The quest of Alroy, however, never left Disraeli, although it was
often reinterpreted and even sublimated in his works. In *Alroy* we
see the first overt statement of Disraeli's "racism" and the first
implied statement of his medievalism. For Disraeli, there is an
inevitability in his ancient race; from the depths of Judaism will
come the salvation of man: "the time will come when from out
our ancient seed, a worthier chief will rise. . . ." The spirit of
history, for Disraeli, is the working out of that salvation. Furthermore, the placement of *Alroy* in the Middle Ages is not mere
accident. As I point out at some length in the next chapter, the
medieval religious view is significant for Disraeli because there
had then taken place a synthesis between Judaism and Christianity, the Hebraeo-Christian Church. The union between the
God of the Old Testament and of the New Testament, between
Disraeli's ancestors and the early church fathers, which produced
the God of Sinai and of Calvary, also produced the religious, political, and societal patterns whose working out in future ages
was the ultimate stuff of history. Just as Coleridge desired to show
that history was a process "governed by the consciousness of
laws," so Disraeli believed that the process of history was the

working out of the spirit of the Hebraeo-Christian Church. Like the Germano-Coleridgeans, Disraeli and his fictional heroes "were looking for a knowledge of the past which might suggest lines of action in the present."[10]

Disraeli, who saw the state as an organic structure and history as a living continuum, conceived of history as moving in a spiraling motion toward the fulfillment of the law of the God of Sinai and of Calvary, which law embraced all areas of man's life. I have said that in each of the novels of the Young England trilogy, the organic, spiraling nature of history is illustrated as the past significantly influences the present and the future and that Disraeli deals with the three principal areas of societal, political, and religious organization. We see that, over and over again, the spirit of the principles and often the principles themselves which Disraeli's protagonists come to accept are medieval in nature. Just as there is an apostolic succession in religion, so we see such a tradition in operation in secular areas of life, a tradition which for Young England must be re-asserted and followed.

Coningsby and *Sybil* interpret this tradition in the areas of social organization and statecraft. In both novels, the disciples of the Young England movement come to see that there are no principles guiding English life, and they sincerely lament this fact. Through an educative process carefully constructed by the author, they come to realize the validity of the medieval ethos; and they attempt to implement the best of it in their own age. In *Tancred*, Disraeli shifts the focus from politics to religion. The possibility of a political solution to England's great ills has reached an impasse, for the proponents of Young England are unfortunately in the distinct minority. Thus the author has Tancred move to an area greater than politics but one which must include politics. Tancred goes to Palestine to seek the answer to the great Asian mystery, an answer which solidifies the basis of Disraeli's views of the Hebraeo-Christian Progress and the organic nature of society. Just as in the Middle Ages, government must follow the lead of the Church if the law-giver is to interpret the Law, so in *Tancred* the solution to the "condition of England" question is given its ultimate statement which involves a union between West and East. In each of the three novels, we see illustrated in imaginative form Disraeli's general position that is outlined in this chapter.

II   Coningsby, Sybil, *and History*

In *Coningsby* and *Sybil*, Coningsby and Egremont come to realize the validity of the providential view of history. They accept the *idea of becoming* in the sweep of history as they transcend the dominant ethics of their time and their social class and move to a Burkean reliance on the great principles of the past as Disraeli brings his heroes to the medievally oriented position of Young England. They respond to the efficacy of the *hero*, that individual who can pierce into the realm of Kant's noumena (or Coleridge's Idea); and, for Disraeli, the heart of noumena beats in the medieval past. The hierarchical, societal arrangement of the Middle Ages is seen by Coningsby and Egremont to be superior to both the Old Toryism's *status quo* and to the Utilitarians' greatest good philosophy. Since the hierarchical arrangement is but a corollary of the great "chain of being" and of the concept of the harmonious nature of existence, it must be *the* social and political pattern to be fulfilled in the course of history. The ethos of the Church of the Middle Ages, with Disraeli's Hebraic ramifications, is accepted by Coningsby and Egremont, although the two novels dwell upon the social and political rather than the religious area of life.

We can already see that Disraeli's philosophy of historical development is, broadly conceived, a Christian one. He does, however, alter the traditionally accepted developmental theory. "The developmental theory . . . was built upon the assumption that the power of a state was wielded successively by an aristocracy of blood, a financial aristocracy, and finally by the populace. The critical stages in history were those which witnessed the transfer of power from one group to another: the final crisis being marked by the transfer of power from property to a populace which had not the ability to govern."[11] Relying on the ancient principles once again, Disraeli would have the development go on without the transfer of power. The aristocracy, through a dedicated application of a Hebraeo-Christian *noblesse oblige*, must remain in control, although Disraeli does allow the financial aristocracy to join the one of blood. Thus the hierarchy remains intact and the problem of critical transfer of power is avoided.

Furthermore, Disraeli believes that a transfer of power to the populace would be a disaster as well as a violation of the spirit of his historical view (see Egremont's impassioned speech on this subject to Sybil—*Sybil*, 321-22). Since the state and its leaders are theoretically moral, there is no danger of a subversion of the rights and blessings due the populace. Here Disraeli agrees with Coleridge, Thomas Arnold, and Julius Hare who also believed that the state must be moral: "In a certain sense these men are statists: the state, because it influences the character of its citizens, is obligated to create, in so far as it can, an environment conducive to the moral development of its individual members."[12] This moral development can take place only when the ruling classes are ideologically committed to the great principles of the past. Disraeli, however, escapes the pessimism which Arnold and Hare came to feel about the future.[13]

As we have seen, Disraeli presents the ideological foundation for his Young England group in *Coningsby*. In this sense *Coningsby* is a novel of theory; in *Sybil*, on the other hand, that theory is put into practice—and is not wholly successful. Tancred and Disraeli come to realize that the working out of the Law, of the Idea, of that which resides in the world of noumena cannot be accomplished through political means alone. A mere handful of inspired statesmen cannot overcome the dominant sociopolitical ethic; and for this reason Tancred spurns a political career and preferment and instead enters upon a pilgrimage to the Holy Land. Like David Alroy, Tancred undergoes a supernatural epiphany in Palestine and is shown that his mission is just and right.

In the greater terms of this discussion, the heavenly visitation to Tancred reinforces the view of history held by his creator, Disraeli. Tancred's pessimism is therefore defeated by the very facts of his world view, by the providential idea of "becoming" in the spirit of history. Hare and Arnold, by analogy, went only as far as Tancred had gone before he went on his crusade. They, Coleridge, and the Germans expected that the spirit of history would be enunciated by the political institutions and laws and that the first estate would aid in the development. Disraeli came to realize that the first estate working through the second and the third was the only way by which the pattern of history could be unfolded. In the ultimate analysis, the Law of the God of Sinai and of Calvary must be the source for all other laws. In my analysis of the Young England trilogy, we can see the precise terms of Disraeli's realization.

III *Disraeli's View of History*

Alfred Cobban has said of Coleridge that "he had learnt to subordinate history to philosophy, and to discover in the historic process only the evolution of a philosophically conceived idea."[14] This same comment can be made of Disraeli when discussing his view of history,[15] a view which cannot be verified on historical grounds. Often, he moves solely in the rarefied atmosphere of historical principle, of his reading of the spirit of history. Almost always, he moves in a historical frame of reference at odds with his time. When Jeremy Bentham claimed that history could show no laws of development and that organic theories of history and the state led to political reaction, he was certainly more the spokesman for nineteenth-century England than was Disraeli with his providential, "becoming" motion in history. Yet Disraeli looked beneath the moral and ethical turmoil of his age and perceived a deep spiritual crisis. That profound awareness stemmed from Disraeli's view of history and of the great principles which he saw in the past. If Disraeli found little articulation of these views in his own time, he would have found much more in ours. Karl Löwith, Jacques Maritain, and Carl Becker, for example, have commented on many of the historical problems which interested Disraeli; and by viewing their responses to the question of meaning in history, we can better grasp Disraeli's view.

Karl Löwith has indicated that the historical view of man "became predominant only in the nineteenth century, but its roots stretch back into the Christian understanding of the universe as a creation, that is, as a universe created *once* for a final purpose and end. Only within such a supra-historical and yet temporal scheme can and must all events be related to their beginning and end, apart from which historical continuity does not make sense."[16] Löwith claims that "the idea of progress could become the leading principle for the understanding of history only within this primary horizon of the future as established by Jewish and Christian faith, against the hopeless, because cyclic, world view of classical paganism."[17] Jacques Maritain, in speaking of the philosophy of history, very closely approximates the heart of Disraeli's world-view. Discussing the divine plan of existence, Maritain states:

But when we deal with the world of freedom, and not only with the world of nature, when we deal with free existents, creatures endowed with freedom of choice, we must go still farther. We must say that in a certain fashion those creatures have their part in the very establishment of the eternal plan—not, indeed, by virtue of their power to act (here all they have they hold of God) but by virtue of their power to nihilate, to make the thing that is nothing, where they themselves . . . are first causes.

The true conception is that the divine plan is immutable *once fixed* from all eternity. But it is only fixed from all eternity *with account taken of the free default of man*, which God sees in His eternal present. Man enters thus into the eternal plan. Not in order to modify it! To say this would be an absurdity. . . .

Thus we can form some idea of the drama of history, or rather the drama of the superior, the sacred regions of history. Whatever is the part of the visible material which conditions it in the world of nature, history is made up above all of the crossing and intermingling, of the pursuit and conflict of created liberty and uncreated liberty [i.e., man's acting with or against the divine plan].[18]

Both Löwith and Maritain are significant because Disraeli's view of history is deeply rooted in religion. Löwith, in general terms, indicates the broad features of a view of progress steeped in the Christian tradition—a view by definition opposed to cyclical theories. Maritain looks at progress and the flow of history within a more precisely defined dialectic. He has announced that there is indeed truth in Burke's belief that mankind's progress is "the known march of the ordinary providence of God." He reinforces Disraeli's view that mankind moves in a spiraling, forward motion up from but always based upon the Law as embedded in Hebraeo-Christianity. Maritain further lends his support to Disraeli's qualification of this spiraling process in that he thinks that it is often checked by a counter-flow created by man out of tune with the well-springs of the world of noumena, by Maritain's "uncreated liberty."

It is impossible for the cyclical view of history and progress to be compatible with Disraeli's theorizing because, for him, there is but *one* cycle! The cyclical view indicates complete revolutions of birth, maturity, and decay, with the pattern repeating itself over and over. Disraeli would agree with Carl Becker who claimed that, "rationally considered, the idea of progress is always at war with its premises."[19] What Becker means is that any view of progress which is rooted in the physical and material human condition must be discarded at the completion of its purpose. Therefore, the theory of progress as an answer to the fundamental and often insoluble questions of man must be unsatisfactory, for only when progress is rooted in the religious situation can answers more satisfying to the human sensibility be found to these great questions: "Why and for what purpose this brief and precarious existence in a universe that endures? What is man's relation to the universe that is sometimes friendly, sometimes hostile, but in the end always fatal to him? How may he elude its hostility, win its favor, find compensations for the intolerable certainty of the death which it will inflict upon him?"[20]

We have seen that there is no ultimate hope offered by the cyclical theories of progress. Becker has this to say of the Christian view of progress: "The strength of the Christian version was that, conceiving human history as a cosmic drama in which all men played their predestined part, it offered to all the hope of eternal life as a compensation for the frustrations of temporal existence: by transferring the golden age from the past to the future it substituted an optimistic for a disillusioned view of human destiny."[21] Disraeli, who seized upon this Hebraeo-Christian view of Progress, built his model of society on the this-worldly aspect of the Christian version. Man must exercise his "created liberty" and thereby aid in the fulfillment of the divine plan, of the Law. In the past—primarily in the Middle Ages—Disraeli saw in action the principles of implementing the Law. The time of the Hebrew-Christian amalgam offers the truest spiritual guide for man. Sidonia announces that "the passionate and creative genius that is the nearest link to divinity, and which no human tyranny can destroy, though it can divert it [through

BENJAMIN DISRAELI

the use of uncreated liberty]; that should have stirred the hearts
of nations by its inspired sympathy, or governed senates by its
burning eloquence, has found a medium for its expression . . ."
(*Coningsby*, 267). That medium is the Hebrew race in conjunction with the early Church: Disraeli's Hebraeo-Christianity.

In passing, we have looked briefly at Edmund Burke, who
stands as a bulwark in support of this organic conception of
history. Burke's conception of the People makes it essential that
"the whole progress of man is . . . dependent, not only on the
historical community in an abstract sense, but on the nature of
the particular community into which he has been born. No man
can abstract himself from this; nor is it his alone to change."[22]
Burke's theory of the organic development of civilization states
in its simplest terms that the present is but an extension of the
past, and that there is an organic, living relationship between
the past, present, and future. Raymond Williams points out that,
for Burke, "art is man's nature"—the artificial society (rather than
the natural) that is necessary to humanize and civilize man.

That this is Burke's position is true, but it is his position
starkly drawn. Williams, however, adds the necessary qualifications when he states that for Burke there was nothing "accidental"
about the particular form of the real society; for "the progress
of human society was 'the known march of the ordinary provi-
dences of God'; the inherited form was divine in origin and guidance, the instrument of God's will that man should become
perfect."[23] Thus, in Burke's view of the organic sweep in history,
man must be forever moving in a spiraling manner toward a
state more and more approaching perfection through a reliance
upon the Natural Law as interpreted by the Church and, in turn,
by the state. The Natural Law comprises, among other things,
those great principles which we see delineated in Disraeli's views
of society, politics, and religion.

As R. G. Collingwood has pointed out in speaking of modern
historical analysis, the medieval view of history—one not unlike
Burke's—has become more and more prevalent in contemporary
historiography:

We have so far gone back to the medieval view of history that we
think of nations and civilizations as rising and falling in obedience

[98]

to a law that has little to do with the purposes of the human beings that comprise them, and we are perhaps not altogether ill-disposed to theories which teach that large-scale historical changes are due to some kind of dialectic working objectively and shaping the historical process by a necessity that does not depend on the human will.[24]

Burke, Coleridge, Carlyle, and Disraeli add to this view the urgency of man's ability to interpret the dialectic of the Law. In the latter three men's philosophies, there are individuals (heroes) in tune with the realm of that dialectic; and they are therefore able to guide the great majority of their fellows by announcing to them and by educating them to the necessity of obeying the great principles.

CHAPTER 5

Society and Religion:
The Young England Novels

DISRAELI and the Young England movement placed enormous concern upon problems that today would be considered broadly within the area of social welfare. This concern struck across narrowly conceived class strata to embrace all classes since England as a unity was at the heart of Young England's crusade. From a desire to elevate the lot of the lowest class to a fervent belief in the social and political efficacy of *noblesse oblige* on the part of the highest class, the adherents of Young England moved up and down the levels of their hierarchically conceived society. We have seen that many of their beliefs in the area of political theory and organization were medieval in nature, but perhaps even more basic to their credo than political medievalism was religious medievalism. With the Church as model and guide, Disraeli and his group felt that the rest could be more easily managed.

We know, of course, that in the Middle Ages there was a close inter-relationship between politics or statecraft and religion; indeed, it is not an overstatement to say that statecraft was but one area of religion. The notion of separation of church and state was theoretical at best; in practice, the two areas were joined together by the same basic framework of duties and obligations and by the same goals. It is no wonder, then, that medieval political philosophers viewed the secular government and its officials as moral agents whose primary duty it was to carry out the Law.

Realizing this oneness of Church and state, we can better appreciate Lewis Mumford's assessment of medieval life: "At a time when actual living was still often brutal, harsh, foolish, and cruel, the Church embodied rationality and ideal purpose: it gave collective dignity to human life at large as no other institution had ever done for so large a part of the Western World before. . . . Never, not even in Greece, had any previous Western society been more completely dominated by respect for the spirit and respect for the authority of those who represented the spirit."[1] The secular representatives of this ecclesiastical authority were thus inheritors of the respect of the masses. And, in theory, the guiding philosophy of the secular authority had at its heart the desire to elevate the lot of the people.

The spiritual nature of each individual man was recognized by the Church and by the secular government, and thus the degradation of any men by other men was, once again in theory, detested. Similarly, Young England was committed to a program of elevating man spiritually and having him recognize his dignity and, of course, that of his fellow human beings. The Utilitarian concepts of man's economic and political selves were not considered important; indeed, they were viewed as outrageously naïve, and, in the final analysis, as of little real concern. Democracy was false since men were not equal (except, again, in the eyes of their Creator), and the burden of duty and respect fell upon Authority. Not only was there a hierarchy among men, but a fundamental hierarchy was to be seen in Nature; the concept of the "chain of being" permeated medieval doctrine. The medieval Church and state were based upon authority, and that authority was predicated upon an elaborate and binding code of behavior. And this view of authority and this code of behavior vitally influenced Disraeli. Perhaps the most lucid introduction to the influence of religious medievalism upon Disraeli is through an examination of two characters created by him: Eustace Lyle in *Coningsby* and Aubrey St. Lys in *Sybil*.

I *Eustace Lyle and* Coningsby

Coningsby is immediately taken with the looks of Eustace Lyle and is interested in Lyle's statement that he had revived the monastic customs at St. Genevieve, his estate, and that there was an alms-giving twice a week. Coningsby asks Lord Henry about Lyle,

"Oh! I will tell you all about him," said Lord Henry. "He is a great ally of mine, and I think you will like him very much. It is a Roman Catholic family, about the oldest we have in the county, and the wealthiest. You see, Lyle's father was the violent ultra-Whig, and so were all Eustace's guardians; but the moment he came of age, he announced that he should not mix himself up with either of the parties in the county, and that his tenantry might act exactly as they thought fit. My father thinks of course that Lyle is a Conservative, and that he only waits the occasion to come forward, but he is quite wrong. I know Lyle well, and he speaks to me without disguise. You see 'tis an old Cavalier family, and Lyle has all the opinions and feelings of his race. He will not ally himself with anti-monarchists, and democrats, and infidels, and sectarians; at the same time why should he support a party who pretend to oppose these, but who never lose an opportunity of insulting his religion, and would deprive him, if possible, of the advantages of the very institutions which his family assisted in establishing?" (*Coningsby*, 146-47)

As Lord Henry continues, he mentions in passing that Lyle is immensely popular in the county and "does an amazing deal of good."

When Coningsby and his companions visit St. Genevieve, they are amazed and at the same time emotionally overwhelmed and delighted as they see in action the medieval religious past. Interestingly enough, Lyle's estate, says Disraeli, was in the finest style of Christian architecture; indeed, St. Genevieve was Augustus Pugin's dream come true. Kenneth Clark reminds us that "there were many sympathetic students of the Middle Ages before Pugin, and many who love to dwell on the courage and piety of its great men. But their attitude was, in the simplest sense, romantic; they loved the middle age as something remote and unconnected with their ordinary lives. To Pugin, however, the life of the Middle Ages was not strange or impossible, but the only good life. He looked on its social structure as a model by which contemporary society must be reformed; and only when the piety and public spirit of that time were re-established could a true Christian architecture arise."[2] At St. Genevieve there was present, therefore, not only the Christian architecture but a society oriented around the medieval religious and social structure.

As they [Lyle, Coningsby, and party] approached the brow of the
hill, that hung over St. Genevieve, they heard the great bell sound.
  "What is that?" asked the duchess.
  "It is almsgiving day," replied Mr. Lyle. . . . "The people of the
parishes with which I am connected come to St. Genevieve twice a
week at this hour."
  "And what is your system?" inquired Lord Everingham, who had
stopped, interested by the scene. "What check have you?"
  "The rectors of the different parishes grant certificates to those who
in their belief merit bounty according to the rules which I have established. These again are visited by my almoner, who countersigns the
certificate and then they present it at the postern-gate. The certificate
explains the nature of their necessities, and my steward acts on his
discretion. . . . Perhaps your grace may think that they might be
relieved without all this ceremony. . . . But I agree . . . that ceremony
is not, as too commonly supposed, an idle form; I wish the people
constantly and visibly to comprehend that property is their protector
and their friend." (*Coningsby*, 153)

On almsgiving day, the pilgrims who came in response to the
great bell are the vassals of Lyle. Disraeli describes the old and
the young who approach carrying their baskets and who are
happy in the security of their position. They are like the workers
of Mr. Trafford; for we are told that there was "not a heart there
. . . did not bless the bell that sounded from the tower of St.
Genevieve" (*Coningsby*, 154).
  Lord Everingham, the ultra-conservative Tory, not only failed
to perceive any sense in the almsgiving but scorned ceremony
in general. To the comment made by Lord Henry that all beauty
has gone out of the modern world, Everingham replies that beauty
may be gone, but life is much easier. Henry, who violently disagrees, announces that "life appears to me to be a fierce struggle
. . . and I wish to see things exactly the reverse. . . . The means
and modes of subsistence less difficult; the conduct of life more
ceremonious" (*Coningsby*, 150). Everingham's only comment is
that "civilisation has no time for ceremony" (151). The question
of ceremony and ritual and their relationship to imagination is
dealt with at some length in *Sybil* and *Tancred*, which we shall
examine later; but in *Coningsby*, directly juxtaposed with Everingham's denial of the value of form, is a description of Lyle's

chapel. Immediately after Everingham's statement, Coningsby and company enter the chapel, one "in which art had exhausted all its invention, and wealth offered all its resources":

The walls and vaulted roofs entirely painted in encaustic by the first artists of Germany, and representing the principal events of the second Testament, the splendour of the mosaic pavement, the richness of the painted windows, the sumptuousness of the altar, crowned by a masterpice of Carlo Dolce and surrounded by a silver rail, the tone of rich and solemn light that pervaded all, and blended all the various sources of beauty into one absorbing and harmonious whole; all combined to produce an effect that stilled them [the visitors] into a silence that lasted for some minutes, until the ladies breathed their feelings in an almost inarticulate murmur of reverence and admiration; while a tear stole to the eye of the enthusiastic Henry Sydney. (*Coningsby*, 150-51)

Without any explicit comment, Disraeli has effectively made clear his view of form and ceremony.

Certainly the rationale underlying such a chapel is precisely the same as that which motivated the great and sacred art of the Middle Ages. "Where art was omnipresent, man could not be altogether vile. In his esthetic consciousness, the medieval craftsman, even the dumb peasant, lived on a higher level than his modern counterpart: his feelings were more fully developed if his intellect was less sharp; and though his domestic life was coarse his public functions were often magnificent, for he daily had the experience of a sacred art which as yet did nothing to sacrifice its austerity or its depth in order to meet a degraded popular demand. . . ."[3] Lyle has successfully transplanted the basic framework of medieval religion into the nineteenth century, and he scorns the Conservative party which ought to have led by great principles but did not: "But there is not a statesman among these Conservatives who offers us a dogma for a guide, or defines any great political truth which we should aspire to establish. It seems to me a barren thing—this Conservatism—an unhappy cross-breed, the mule of politics that engenders nothing" (*Coningsby*, 155). Lyle has risen above party and has invoked the Middle Ages, a time in which he saw the dogma by which man can be guided. In an age lacking principles, Lyle re-established in his small corner of England the leadership through principles which Disraeli clearly admired.

St. Genevieve and the village of Trafford have much in common, but perhaps the most striking feature of each is that no semblance of democracy is present. Just as the Middle Ages rested firmly on an authoritarian hierarchy, so do Lyle's and Trafford's domains. In each we can see re-enacted the spiritual, political, and social drama of feudal England (always, again, as the Young England movement romanticized that drama). The people were happy and secure within an undemocratic, hierarchical pattern—a thought which Young England realized was inconceivable to many of their Utilitarian opponents. Democracy, indeed, was actively distrusted and openly held to be invalid in terms of man's most significant and meaningful needs and desires. Coningsby believes that democracy breeds not only a neglected people but legislation by and for the more educated or politically successful classes. The only powers which have no class sympathies, he feels, are the sovereign and the Church; for the sovereign, responsible for the people and guided by the great principles of the Church, must act in a manner beneficial to *all* classes, to all the people.

Furthermore, the sovereign and the Church are beyond the sphere of influence of either an indifferent or a corrupt public opinion; and Disraeli intimates that the people must be aided whether or not they like it at first. He has no doubt that by means of the Church's acting through its representatives in the political and social areas, all men can come to be as happy in life as those at St. Genevieve and Trafford: "The estate of the Church is the estate of the people, as long as the Church is governed on its real principles" (*Coningsby*, 378). At St. Genevieve Disraeli presents the Church as governed by real principles; the people, as thriving:

It was merry Christmas at St. Genevieve. There was a Yule log blazing on every hearth in that wide domain, from the hall of the squire to the peasant's roof. The buttery hatch was open for the whole week from noon to sunset; all comers might take their fill, and each carry away as much bold beef, white bread, and jolly ale as a strong man could bear in a basket with one hand. For every woman a red cloak, and a coat of broadcloth for every man. All day long, carts laden with fuel and warm raiment were traversing the various districts, distributing comfort and dispensing cheer. For a Christian gentleman of high degree was Eustace Lyle.

Within his hall too he holds his revel, and his beauteous bride welcomes their guests from her noble parents to the faithful tenants of the house. All classes are mingled in the joyous equality that becomes the season, at once sacred and merry. (*Coningsby*, 463)

Lyle's behavior compares with the following estimate of the medieval Church's greatest gifts as beauty and fellowship:

Once a week at least . . . every member of the community had a glimpse of the highest life possible: lord and peasant, master and journeyman, lady and wench, worshipped together in the same buildings, watched and took part in the same processions, heard the same chants, beheld the same icons, listened to the same sermons, followed the same mass: all equal in the sight and presence of God. On earth their lots were unequal. . . . But in Heaven, worldly advantages and disadvantages were nullified; and the Church itself, by its very ministrations, stood in the relationship of that Earthly Paradise which was the last stage in Purgatory on the way to Heaven.[4]

In the sight of Lyle and Disraeli, the Church, guided by true principles, could never lose this sympathy for the poor. By virtue of these principles, the Church was aware that man needed more than the "bed and board" of Abbot Hugo.

Disraeli constructs his novels so that his protagonists become aware of the fact "that a mere mechanical mitigation of the material necessities of the humbler classes, a mitigation which must inevitably be very limited, can never alone avail sufficiently to ameliorate their condition; that their condition is not merely a 'knife and fork question,' to use the coarse and shallow phrase of the Utilitarian school; that a simple satisfaction of the grosser necessities of our nature will not make a happy people; that you must cultivate the heart as well as seek to content the belly . . ." (*Coningsby*, 464). So at St. Genevieve in *Coningsby* Disraeli gives us a first, clear intimation of a religious medievalism which he develops in *Sybil* and brings to fruition in *Tancred*.

II *Aubrey St. Lys and* Sybil

In the process of Egremont's growth throughout *Sybil*, Aubrey
St. Lys' influence is not inconsiderable. Immediately before St.
Lys is given the center of the stage, Egremont comments that he
has been thinking "of late about these things; monasteries and
so on: the influence of the old Church system on the happiness
and comfort of the People" (*Sybil*, 123). In terms of the structure
of the novel, this utterance is significant because St. Lys is the
younger son of the oldest Norman family in England. A dedicated man of Lyle's cut, St. Lys has all that he desires: he is
the vicar of Mowbray. His beautiful cathedral, rising in the midst
of the ugly industrial town of Mowbray and surrounded by the
toiling, teeming thousands of workers, acts as a fountainhead for
Disraeli's discussion of religion.

Ironically, this remnant of a religion long forgotten by the
"hundred thousand heathen" of the area indirectly brings Mowbray to its present position of industrial prosperity. The "magnificent temple" had been built by the monks of Mowbray; and,
although the sanctity and morality for which the building stood
are no longer meaningful, the building remains. "And so it was
. . . when manufacturers were introduced into this district,
which abounded with all the qualities necessary for their successful pursuit, to Mowbray, offering equal though not superior
advantages to other positions, was accorded the preference, 'because it possessed such a beautiful church'" (*Sybil*, 125). The
church of St. Lys is perfectly symbolic, and the plight of the
cathedral clearly mirrors the condition of England's religious
life. This life is composed of only external and superficial concepts; it is a religion devoted to the extrinsic rather than the
intrinsic, to buildings rather than principles. The mission of St.
Lys is, therefore, to preach the "Unknown God." Where Trafford
and Lyle create cultures in the medieval mold, St. Lys is faced
with the perhaps greater task of remolding a "wayward culture."

St. Lys is guided and inspired by his (and Disraeli's) conception of the Church: the Hebraeo-Christian Church. As will become more and more evident, Disraeli's religious medievalism is
not without certain *refinements* peculiar to Disraeli. One of these

—and perhaps the major one—is first introduced by St. Lys to Egremont when they are discussing the efficacy of forms and ceremonies. St. Lys has announced that religion had once satisfied the wants and needs of man:

Its festivals relieved the painful weariness of toil. The day of rest was consecrated, if not always to elevated thought, at least to sweet and noble sentiments. The Church convened to its solemnities, under its splendid and almost celestial roofs, amid the finest monuments of art that human hands have raised, the whole Christian population; for there, in the presence of God, all were brethren. It shared equally among all its prayers, its incense, and its music; its sacred institutions, and the highest enjoyments that the arts could afford. (*Sybil*, 129)

When Egremont asks St. Lys if he truly believes in forms and ceremonies, the vicar answers: "What you call forms and ceremonies represent the divinest instincts of our nature" (*Sybil*, 129). When Egremont (not yet a fully developed member of Young England) pursues the point by suggesting that many Englishmen associate ceremony with "enthralling superstition and a foreign dominion," St. Lys enunciates the conception of the Hebraeo-Christian Church:

The Church of Rome is to be respected as the only Hebraeo-Christian Church extant; all other churches established by the Hebrew apostles have disappeared, but Rome remains; and we must never permit the exaggerated position which it assumed in the middle centuries [St. Lys believes in a clean division between church and state, albeit his state would be oriented about religious principles] to make us forget its early and apostolical character, when it was fresh from Palestine, and as it were fragrant from Paradise. The Church of Rome is sustained by apostolical succession; but apostolical succession is not an institution complete in itself; it is a part of a whole; if it be not part of a whole it has no foundation. The apostles succeeded the prophets. Our Master announced Himself as the last of the prophets. They in turn were the heirs of the patriarchs: men who were in direct communication with the Most High. To men not less favoured than the apostles, the revelation of the priestly character was made, and those forms and ceremonies ordained, which the Church of Rome has never relinquished. But Rome did not invent them: upon their practice, the duty of all congregations, we cannot consent to her founding a claim to supremacy. For would you maintain then that the

Church did not exist in the time of the prophets? Was Moses then
not a Churchman? And Aaron, was he not a high priest? . . . In all
these Church discussions, we are apt to forget that the second Testament is avowedly only a supplement. Jehovah-Jesus came to complete
the "law and the prophets." Christianity is completed Judaism, or it
is nothing. Christianity is incomprehensible without Judaism, as Judaism is incomplete without Christianity. . . . I recognize in the Church
an institution thoroughly, sincerely catholic: adapted to all climes,
and to all ages. I do not bow to the necessity of a visible head in a
defined locality; but were I to seek for such, it would not be at Rome.
I cannot discover in its history, however memorable, any testimony
of a mission so sublime. When Omnipotence deigned to be incarnate,
the Ineffable Word did not select a Roman frame. The prophets were
not Romans; the Apostles were not Romans; she, who was blessed
above all women, I never heard she was a Roman maiden. No, I
should look to a land more distant than Italy, to a city more sacred
even than Rome. (*Sybil*, 130-31)

What we see in this statement, in addition to the Hebraeo-
Christian concept but overriding it, is Disraeli's deep sense of
historical tradition. *The* tradition, of which the present is only
the latest appendage, is so great that both the Middle Ages and
the Roman Catholic Church become but segments of that organic,
spiraling continuum. In the areas of politics, social organization,
and religious organization, the time of the Middle Ages offered
the models by which Disraeli could pattern his world-view; but
the theoretical, spiritual foundation for these "practical" applications are seen to be far older than even the Middle Ages.

Alfred North Whitehead has suggested that "the Hebrews
had no independent state to govern, and a man cannot be
blamed for failing to consider what there was in his period
no occasion for considering. He [Jesus] said what an able
thinker might be expected to say. His historical situation did
not elicit a code of ethics concerned with responsibility for a
social system. . . . It [Christianity] held that the externals of
life are not worth caring about and at the same time insisted on
types of moral conduct which cannot be observed—without per-
ishing—unless the externals of life are sufficiently well organized.
A society run on strictly Christian principles could not survive
at all."[5] Whitehead focuses attention upon a crucial element
within Disraeli's view of tradition. At the time of the transition

from Hebrew to Christian, there were no established principles of social, political, or religious organization. Present, however, was the entire spiritual framework which ultimately was used as the basis for establishing the organizational elements. It is, then, the blending of the Hebraic with the Christian which produced the tradition within which Disraeli operates.

In addition to being the first of Disraeli's characters to clearly articulate the Hebraeo-Christian religious concept, St. Lys reinforces the need for ceremony and form; and he also re-emphasizes the sympathetic relationship of the Church with the poor (essentially the same relationship which Young England felt must exist between the aristocracy and the poor). We remember Lyle's view of ceremony as we recall St. Lys's discussion of ritual with Egremont. In *Sybil*, the subject of ceremony is introduced as a leitmotif and woven throughout the novel. In addition to a discussion of ceremony in purely religious terms of the kind we have seen in *Coningsby* and *Sybil*, Disraeli also handles the subject within a lay framework. At a "monster meeting" of laborers at a moor outside Mowbray, a portion of the festivities is described in these terms:

Sometimes a large party arrived without music or banners, but singing psalms, and headed by their minister; sometimes the children walked together, the women following, then the men each with a ribbon of the same colour in his hat; all hurried, yet spontaneous and certain, indications how mankind, under the influence of high and earnest feelings, recur instantly to ceremony and form; how, when the imagination is excited, it appeals to the imagination, and requires for its expression something beyond the routine of daily life. (*Sybil*, 394-95)

Initially, and most cogent in the context of the present discussion, we see a strong reinforcement of the efficacy of ceremony. Indeed, by commenting upon the effects of it in this secular situation, Disraeli highlights the subject. And, by coupling ceremony with imagination, Disraeli completes a full circle of theory and brings the entire area of ceremony back to the tenets of Young England and the new Toryism. One of those tenets urged vigorously that more than bed and board was needed if man was to approach the status demanded for him by the Natural Law. If, then, Disraeli now announces a relation-

ship between ceremony and imagination and, indeed, adds that
the expression of the imagination requires "something beyond
the routine of daily life," is he not once more refuting Abbot
Hugo's philosophy in favor of Abbot Samson's? More is necessary
for man's *real* welfare than the extrinsic goals proposed by the
Utilitarians.

One aspect of man's intrinsic nature can be expressed through
ceremony, form and ritual—in short, through those agents which
nourish the imagination. Disraeli has indicated through the
workers' rally the fact that ceremony and imagination need not
be the exclusive domain of religion; they can be effectively in-
corporated in the secular lives of the people. In fact, do we not
see ceremony and imagination infusing and permeating all aspects
of Disraeli's reading of medieval life? Do we not see the same
attitude in Trafford's village, as well as in Lyle's St. Genevieve?
And we now see it in Mowbray at a workers' rally.

Yet we must point out that even within the secular framework
of the workers' rally, the essential tone of the ceremonies involved
is a religious one. The processions, the psalms, the minister at
the head, the decorum and formality, and the "congregation's"
regulated participation in the "service" are all postures of the
religious ceremony. It is the religious life which becomes the
well-spring for all other facets of life. Just as there is, in religious
terms, an ultimate leader, one to whom the service is directed
by other and lesser leaders on the hierarchical scale, so in the
terms of the workers' rally there is a secular leader around whom
the masses have gathered and to whom they look for guidance
and, indeed, for deliverance. Sidonia's comment about man's need
to adore and obey takes on added significance as we observe
the workers' elaborate preparations for the arrival of Walter
Gerard; for the attitudes of worship and respect for authority
which underscore this scene are precisely those which we have
previously seen in *Coningsby* when the new MP was greeted by
adoring crowds at Darlford. Thus coupled together in one relatively brief scene are ceremony, imagination, and the conception
of the hero in a secular situation, which in the final analysis
comes to be seen as fundamentally a religious situation—or, at
least, certainly as an organic extension of it.

III *The Aristocracy and the Church*

The Church, acting in its own right as well as through an aware aristocracy, was at the heart of the liaison between the uppermost and lowest classes. We have already seen Egremont's plea to Sybil in which the young nobleman announced a cardinal fact of Disraeli's view: the aristocracy must and would rescue the lower classes and all of England. As a matter of fact, Walter Gerard himself is discovered to be an aristocrat, a realization which heightens this aspect of Egremont-Disraeli's view. That Egremont was influenced and moved by the Church need not be elaborated any further. In *Sybil* we see the Church acting its role as caretaker of the entire nation.

Disraeli "loads the deck" in order to illustrate—and sometimes over-illustrate—the plight of the people. The scenes of domestic misery, for example, of old Warner's family must have rent many Victorian hearts. The people are in a state of degradation, says Walter Gerard to Egremont:

"There is more serfdom in England now than at any time since the Conquest. I speak of what passes under my daily eyes when I say, that those who labour can as little choose or change their masters now, as when they were born thralls. There are great bodies of the working classes of this country nearer the condition of brutes than they have been at any time since the Conquest. Indeed I see nothing to distinguish them from brutes, except that their morals are inferior. Incest and infanticide are as common among them as among the lower animals. The domestic principle wanes weaker and weaker every year in England; nor can we wonder at it, when there is not comfort to cheer and no sentiment to hallow the Home." (*Sybil*, 199-200)

There is little wonder that *Sybil* was a popular seller and that Disraeli found a sympathetic audience. The scenes of human degeneracy in the town of Wodgate were found shocking, but they effectively brought home the author's thesis. Disraeli was implying that Wodgate, the logical end product of a culture bent upon impersonal and mechanical progress, is nature perverted: "a population gathered, and rapidly increased, in the ugliest spot in England, to which neither Nature nor Art had contributed a single charm; where a tree could not be seen, a flower was unknown, where there was neither belfry nor steeple, nor a single sight or sound that could soften the heart or humanize the mind" (*Sybil*, 188). The landscape, like that of a circle within Dante's Inferno, is the symbolic retribution for those who pursued the cash-payment, "bed and board" philosophy of Abbot Hugo.

But Wodgate is also religion perverted: " 'Yes, sir,' said the girl [a native of Wodgate discussing her new husband and her religious beliefs]. . . . 'I be a reg'lar born Christian and my mother afore me, and that's what few gals in the Yard can say. Thomas will take to it himself when work is slack; and he believes now in our Lord and Saviour Pontius Pilate, who was crucified to save our sins; and in Moses, Goliath, and the rest of the Apostles'" (*Sybil*, 194). As an additional comment on the perverted state of religion, the Lord's Prayer is recited backwards in Wodgate. The pained comment Morley makes upon the condition of this sub-human town looms larger out of the context of the novel and within the ideological context of the Young England movement: "Ah! me, and could not they spare one Missionary from Tahiti for their fellow-countrymen at Wodgate!" (*Sybil*, 194). As if in response, Disraeli's few secular missionaries were forming under the banner of Young England.

In *Sybil*, Disraeli shows only two agencies interested in aiding the poor: the new aristocracy and the Church. The author carefully builds an implied argument which shows (1) the horrifying state of the people, (2) the complacency and smugness of the old and more numerous aristocrats, and (3) the Church's compassion for the plight of the people. (Disraeli would consider the new aristocracy a secular member of the Church.) Sybil herself keynotes the relationship between Church and people when she tells Egremont that "I have lived under two roofs, only two roofs; and each has given me a great idea; the Convent and the Cottage. One has taught me the degradation of my faith, the other of my race. You should not wonder, therefore, that my heart is concentrated on the Church and the People" (*Sybil*, 206). Thus a second pair of crucial terms is introduced. Where there was sharp contrast expressed in the novel's sub-title, "The Two Nations," between the Rich and the Poor, there is a close affinity expressed in this second pair of terms, the Church and the People. Gerard recognizes the fact that at one time in the past, the relationship between Church and People was vital and fruitful: "Ah! if we could only have the Church on our side, as in the good old days, we would soon put an end to the demon of tyranny of Capital" (*Sybil*, 377).

That the Church must once more achieve this same relationship forms one of the tenets of Young England and is given illustration in Disraeli's novels. Even in the midst of England's "fallen condition," the Church attempts to aid the poor. Sybil, Gerard, Egremont, Trafford, Coningsby, St. Lys, and Lyle are all influenced by the Church; and they, in turn, urge it forward. The influence of the Church on individuals is great, implies Disraeli, as in the following description of Lady Maud: "She was all animation—charmed to see everybody; she had been to Mowbray to hear some singing at the Roman Catholic chapel in that town; a service had been performed and a collection made for the suffering work-people of the place" (*Sybil*, 420). The singing had completely enthralled her; the voice was angelic. It was, of course, Sybil's singing. Just as she moved among the houses of the poor, ministering to the wretched inhabitants, bringing a bit of happiness into their sad lives, so she strongly affected the parishioners at church—as, indeed, she had affected Egremont at the monastery ruins.

Sybil reflects the spirit of the Church, and in a conversation between her and a Lady Superior, the Church's relationship to the people is beautifully summed up. In a room "softened by the stained panes of a small Gothic window," as the setting sun came through, the Lady Superior of the Convent of Mowbray says, "That my visions were of the world, and brought me to the cloister, and that yours were of the cloister, and have brought you to the world" (*Sybil*, 423). The interrelationship of the "Convent and the Cottage" is once more enunciated as two individuals, one secular and one religious, stand close to each other in a room within a religious house within an industrial village. The concentric circles of secular life in its many phases flow around their center, the Church.

IV   Tancred *and "The Great Asian Mystery"*

Now that we have seen more clearly the medievalism of Lyle in *Coningsby* and of St. Lys in *Sybil*, we are in a position to

view Disraeli's fullest treatment of the subject as it appears in
Tancred, the most complex of Disraeli's novels. Although this
novel has bewildered many readers, the author himself preferred
it to his other works.[6] Yet even sensitive readers, partial to Disraeli, have had their difficulties with the novel. Sir Leslie Stephen
wrote of "the strange phantasmagoria of *Tancred*,"[7] and Morris
Speare considered *Tancred* "bizarre and incoherent and in-
organic."[8] Most commentators have treated the novel super-
ficially or have ignored it,[9] and *Tancred* has remained in the
dark corner of Disraeli's Young England trilogy. However,
Tancred can be read as a coherent and organic work; and the key
to such a reading is to be found in Disraeli's religious philosophy.

Although Disraeli had informed his readers in The General
Preface that *Tancred* was the third novel in a trilogy, the thematic distance between *Tancred* and *Sybil* is great. Where there
are numerous subjects common to *Coningsby* and *Sybil*, *Tancred*
deals primarily with the area of religion and with the political
and social areas only tangentially, although sharply. In *Tancred*,
when Disraeli discusses political and social matters, he relates
them to the religious base of the novel. Fundamentally, the
novelist's point in both of these areas is that because English
life is motivated by no great principles rooted in the great religion of the past, political and social problems multiply while
solutions become more and more expedient, compromising, and
unsuccessful.

When in the company of several of his contemporaries who
had entered Parliament, Tancred announces his view of their
profession. He tells Lord Henry that "if a Parliamentary career
could save this country, I am sure you would be a public bene-
factor. I have observed what you and Mr. Coningsby and some
of your friends have done and said, with great interest. But Parliament seems to me to be the very place which a man of action
should avoid" (*Tancred*, 140). Tancred continues:

A Parliamentary career, that old superstition of the eighteenth century, was important when there were no other sources of power and
fame. An aristocracy at the head of a people whom they had plundered
of their means of education, required some cultivated tribunal whose
sympathy might stimulate their intelligence and satisfy their vanity.
Parliament was never so great as when they debated with closed

doors. The public opinion, of which they never dreamed, has super-seded the rhetorical club of our great-grandfathers. They know this well-enough, and try to maintain their unnecessary position by affect-ing the character of men of business, but amateur men of business are very costly conveniences. In this age it is not Parliament that does the real work. . . . If the manufacturers want to change a tariff, they form a commercial league, and they effect their purpose. . . . Parliament has become as really insignificant as for two centuries it has kept the monarch. . . . I am inclined to believe . . . that if our order had any spirit of prescience, they would put themselves at the head of the people, and take the rest [i.e., take control]. . . . I go to a land that has never been blessed by that fatal drollery called a representative government, though Omniscience once deigned to trace out the polity which should rule it. (*Tancred*, 140-41)

Not only does Tancred decry the effect and influence of public opinion; he fears it: "I do not see how there can be opinion without thought and I do not believe the public ever think. How can they? They have no time" (*Tancred*, 151). Obviously, if the public's judgments are insincere, if Parliament is controlled by various vested interest groups, and if both the sovereign and the Church are ineffectual vestiges of what they once had been, the very structure of English life is at a point near total collapse.

To account for this variation in Disraeli's theme, we should recall that in *Coningsby* the Young England movement had got underway and that a group of brilliant young MP's were about to assume their places in the practical world of English political life, their theoretical ponderings having been completed. In *Sybil*, Charles Egremont not only placed his trust in the new, enlightened aristocracy's ability to solve the great social prob-lems of his day, but he also carried his views into the very heart of British politics, the Parliament House itself. What, then, has led Disraeli to create a character like Tancred who openly and bluntly scorns the work of government; who indeed feels the efforts of Coningsby and company to be so much wasted time?

One obvious answer is that by 1847 the Young England movement had evaporated. The master no longer had any dis-ciples to instruct. But this situation was only part of the greater reason for Disraeli's shift in thematic development. Certainly, even in *Sybil*, Disraeli is realistic enough to indicate the wide disparity between ideal and real political success. Egremont, in theory, is brilliantly and sensitively correct according to Young England's political ethic. Yet he is far more successful as a theorizer and enunciator of political ideology than he is as a practical mover of political change. Egremont's speech in behalf of the Corn Law Charter succeeded no better than the actual speech upon which it was modeled. Disraeli, like Egremont, was forced to realize that far greater changes must first take place within his country before particular political measures of the Young England type could be embraced by Parliament. An entirely new climate of life must be introduced if the new Toryism was to become a significant party in terms of practical political success.

Another answer to the original problem—and a popular one— is summed up by Monypenny. By 1847, Disraeli had become an important and brilliant politician. Although he had tremendous ambition and was blessed with political genius, he realized that his rise was made more difficult by the prejudice against him: "And *Tancred* strikes the reader less as the accomplishment of a political purpose, than as a sudden revolt by the author against the routine and hollowness of politics, against its prejudice and narrowness; and as an assertion of his detachment and superiority to it all by the glorification of his race and by the proclamation of the mystic ideas, inherited from the Jews, which marked him out from the commonplace mediocrities around him."[10] To be sure, the range of prejudice which surrounded Disraeli was considerable—from the overtly anti-Semitic, distorted biographical pieces to the many songs, limericks, and jingles such as *Jew-de-Brass* or *Dizzi-Ben-Dizzi*.[11] In the face of such crude attack, in addition to the more genteel barbs and slights of many of his peers, it is possible that one major element in *Tancred* is an elaborate defense mechanism on Disraeli's part.

However, it seems to me that by placing so great an emphasis on Disraeli's Hebraeo-Christianity the argument rests upon questionable premises: that Disraeli's father was an active convert from Judaism and that Disraeli himself was an eager convert to Christianity. Speare, who intimates both of these premises, goes so far as to accuse Disraeli of consciously bolstering up "his theories of race with a false ethnology and a still falser anthropology, and that he misquoted the facts of history to prove his somewhat bizarre contentions."[12] It would seem far more judicious to view the subject matter of *Tancred* as a vehicle for Disraeli to present more clearly his views of the Hebraeo-Christian Church, which he had discussed earlier in more diluted form in *Sybil*. Since we do have the testimony for the existence of such a view presented in *Sybil* (and, indeed, in other works like *The Life of Lord George Bentinck*), an examination of its presence in *Tancred*, based upon psychoanalytical premises, is at best of secondary interest.

To fully solve the problem of why *Tancred* departs from the thematic pattern already established in *Coningsby* and *Sybil*, we must assume not only that Disraeli had come to realize that his country was not ready for Young England, but that the new Toryism was predicated upon a culture ideologically far different from England's. A culture in tune with the Hebraeo-Christian Church (as Disraeli imagined it) was necessary before the Young England credo could become meaningful. Since England did not afford such a culture, Young England as a political action movement was stalemated; politics as the means for exerting beneficial change had reached an impasse. Tancred, who had realized this fact, refused his father's suggestion that he enter Parliament. Rather, Tancred turned his eyes toward the East, toward the Holy Land. It was Palestine and the message of religion that Tancred yearned for, not Parliament.[13]

In the opening chapters of *Tancred*, Disraeli presents an excited Duke and Duchess of Montacute. Their county member in Parliament had just informed the Montacutes that he was going to withdraw from Parliament since Tancred, the young Lord Montacute, was now of age: "A Marquis of Montacute is, in my opinion," says the loyal MP, ". . . our proper representative . . ." (*Tancred*, 25). However, Tancred has no desire to enter Parliament. In response to his father's insistence that the son change his mind, Tancred makes clear his disdain for politics and his interest in the spiritual attraction of Asia.

"There would be no necessity, under any circumstances for that [having the present MP remain for the next three years], my dear father," said Lord Montacute, looking up, and speaking in a voice which, though somewhat low, was of that organ that at once arrests

attention: a voice that comes alike from the brain and from the
heart, and seems made to convey both profound thought and deep
emotion. There is no index of character so sure as the voice. There
are tones, tones brilliant and gushing, which impart a quick and
pathetic sensibility: there are others that, deep and yet calm, seem
the just interpreters of a serene and exalted intellect. But the rarest
and most precious of all voices is that which combines passion and
repose; and whose rich and restrained tones exercise, perhaps, on
the human frame a stronger spell than even the fascination of the
eye, or the bewitching influence of the hand, which is the privilege
of the higher races of Asia.

"There would be no necessity, under any circumstances, for that,
my dear father," said Lord Montacute; "for, to be frank, I believe I
should feel as little disposed to enter Parliament three years hence
as now." (*Tancred*, 47)

Not only is the question of Asia introduced, but in this refusal
by Tancred Disraeli sets the stage for the greater drama to be
unveiled in the novel.

One aspect of Tancred's decision not to enter Parliament is
similar to a view that we have already seen presented by both
Coningsby and Egremont. Tancred tells his father that there is
no state guided by meaningful and great principles. "Ah! if any
one would but tell me what the State is. . . . It seems to me
your pillars remain, but they support nothing. . . . They [states-
men] do not even pretend to be a State . . . ; they do not even
profess to support anything; on the contrary, the essence of their
philosophy is, that nothing is to be established, and everything
is to be left to itself" (*Tancred*, 48). Although Tancred agrees
with the sentiments of Coningsby and Egremont, his prescription
for remedying the situation is far more fundamental and broad
than that of his predecessors. Where they turned to Parliament
and political action as remedial agencies, Tancred turns to religion because the cultural base of England must be altered if
proper political action is to be successful. Thus Tancred believes
that the answers which he hopes to find in religion will re-orient
him toward a more effective course of thought and action.
Tancred needs and wants direction; he must discover the world-
view upon which he can base his life, upon which England
can base her life:

"You have proposed to me today . . . to enter public life. I do not shrink from its duties. On the contrary, from the position in which I am born, still more from the impulse of my nature, I am desirous to fulfill them. I have meditated on them, I may say, even for years. But I cannot find that it is part of my duty to maintain the order of things, for I will not call it system, which at present prevails in our country. It seems to me that it cannot last, as nothing can endure, that is not founded upon principle; and its principle I have not discovered. In nothing, whether it be religion, or government, or manners, sacred or political or social life, do I find faith; and if there be no faith, how can there be duty? Is there such a thing as religious truth? Is there such a thing as political right? Is there such a thing as social propriety? Are these facts, or are they mere phrases? And if they be facts, where are they likely to be found in England? Is truth in our Church? Why, then, do you support dissent? Who has the right to govern? The Monarch? You have robbed him of his prerogative. The Aristocracy? You confess to me that we exist by sufferance. The People? They themselves tell you that they are nullities. Every session of that Parliament in which you wish to introduce me, the method by which power is distributed is called in question, altered, patched up, and again impugned. As for our morals, tell me, is charity the supreme virtue, or the greatest of errors? Our social system ought to depend on a clear conception of this point." (*Tancred,* 50-51)

The answers Tancred seeks obviously cannot be found in Parliament; he therefore desires to visit the Holy Land: "In a word, it is the Holy Land that occupies my thought, and I propose to make a pilgrimage to the sepulchre of my Saviour" (*Tancred,* 56). As if symbolically, the Duke is both amazed and appalled at his son's desire. Tancred continues:

"When I remember that the Creator, since light sprang out of darkness, has deigned to reveal Himself to His creature only in one land; that in that land He assumed a manly form, and met a human death; I feel persuaded that the country sanctified by such inter-course and such events must be endowed with marvellous and peculiar qualities, which man may not in all ages be competent to penetrate, but which, nevertheless, at all times exercise an irresistible influence upon his destiny. It is these qualities that many times drew Europe to Asia during the middle centuries. Our castle has before this sent forth a De Montacute to Palestine. For three days and three nights he knelt at the tomb of his Redeemer. Six centuries and more have elapsed since that great enterprise. It is time to restore and renovate our communications with the Most High. I, too, would kneel at that tomb; I, too, surrounded by the holy hills and sacred groves of Jerusalem, would relieve my spirit from the bale that bows it down; would lift up my voice to heaven, and ask, what is DUTY, and what is FAITH? What ought I to DO, and what ought I to BELIEVE?" (*Tancred*, 56)

Tancred is thus to rehearse the spiritual drama of his medieval ancestors.

When the Duke and Duchess attempt to change their son's mind, their attempts run the gamut from having their family clergyman attempt to dissuade their "wayward" son to introducing Tancred into London society in the hope that the glitter of social life will keep him from his mission. Although the latter tempts him, Tancred is not to be denied his crusade. In the course of the dissuasive attempts, however, Disraeli is afforded several opportunities of satirizing and criticizing the English clergy, London high society, and the new scientific ideas of the second quarter of the century.

After the local clergyman's failure to change Tancred's mind, the Duchess calls upon the Bishop—in every way a poor choice. Disraeli's Bishop epitomizes the sickness of the English Church, and the worldly realm he represents must clash with and fail to understand Tancred's spiritual yearning:

He [the Bishop] combined a great talent for action with very limited powers of thought. Bustling, energetic, versatile, gifted with an indomitable perseverance, and stimulated by an ambition that knew no repose, with a capacity for mastering details and an inordinate passion for affairs, he could permit nothing to be done without his interference, and consequently was perpetually involved in transactions which were either failures or blunders. He was one of those leaders who are not guides. Having little real knowledge, and not endowed with those high qualities of intellect which permit their possessor to generalise the details afforded by study and experience, and so deduce rules of conduct, his lordship, when he received those frequent appeals which were the necessary consequence of his officious life, became obscure, confused, contradictory, inconsistent, and illogical. The oracle was always dark. Placed in a high post in an age of political analysis, the bustling intermeddler was unable to supply society with a single solution. Enunciating second-hand, with characteristic precipitation, some big principle in vogue, as if he were a discoverer, he invariably shrank from its subsequent application, the moment that he found it might be unpopular and inconvenient. All his quandaries terminated in the same catastrophe; a compromise. Abstract principles with him ever ended in concrete expediency. (*Tancred*, 74)

This is by no means just a particular Bishop whom Disraeli is describing; he represents the state of religion in England. The irony of such a representative of such a church attempting to dissuade Tancred from his mission is obvious.

The only things necessary for Tancred before he can depart are letters of reference and recommendation, and Disraeli directs the young Lord to Sidonia. Once more Sidonia becomes the instrument by which change is brought about in a young nobleman. And it is Sidonia who introduces the phrase, "the Asian mystery," upon which the remainder of the novel is to turn. In a letter of introduction to Alonza Lara, Spanish Prior, at the Convent of Terra Santa at Jerusalem, Sidonia writes: "MOST HOLY FATHER, The youth who will deliver to you this is a pilgrim who aspires to penetrate the great Asian mystery. Be to him what you were to me; and may the God of Sinai, in whom we all believe, guard over you, and prosper his enterprise!" (*Tancred*, 171). While Disraeli was Prime Minister, a clergyman wrote him seeking the meaning of the "great Asian mystery." Disraeli instructed his private secretary: "Write to this gentleman that, as I have written three volumes [the Young England trilogy] to answer the question he asks, and, as far as he is concerned, have failed, it would be presumption to suppose I could be more fortunate in a letter. Recommend repeated, and frequent, study of the work as the most efficient means for his purpose."[14] Taking Disraeli's advice, we must turn our attention to the details of the "mystery" as they are delineated in the last of the three works.

Once Tancred leaves England, his adventures begin. Upon reaching Bethany, he is overcome by sleep in a beautiful, exotic garden. He awakes to discover Eva, the Rose of Sharon, standing over him. She is a beautiful and brilliant Jewess with whom Tancred falls in love. Coincidentally, Eva is the daughter of the Croesus of Syria, one of Sidonia's acquaintances to whom Tancred carries a letter of introduction. Eva spends some time during this first encounter indoctrinating Tancred into the mysteries and greatness of the Hebrew faith. Tancred travels, visits convents, shrines, and tombs, and seeks spiritual guidance. He meets Fakredeen, a young, eccentric, and perhaps brilliant Emir, who is caught up in political stratagems and dreams. The two young men exchange bits of political philosophy, but Tancred must be on.

He finally reaches the sepulchre of Christ, fasts, prays, but undergoes no spiritual epiphany. Sinai is the next stop on the itinerary, but Tancred and his party are ambushed and taken prisoners by a band of Arabs. Thinking that Tancred is the brother of Queen Victoria, the Arabs hold him for ransom. Fakredeen enters once more and has several fascinating conversations with our hero. Tancred does finally reach Sinai, experiences an angelic visitation, and hears the message of the vision. He then suddenly becomes ill and is nursed back to health by Eva, but they both become captives of the Queen of Ansary, Astarte, whose people still worship the Greek gods of Mount Olympus.

The novel moves to a hopeful conclusion as the central characters escape from Astarte (who has by this time fallen in love with Tancred and has planned to kill Eva), and ends in a tranquil scene in which Eva and Tancred embrace at twilight in the beautiful, exotic garden. Perhaps one critic is correct when he says that Douglas Fairbanks could not improve on the spectacle and adventure which Disraeli has packed into his novel.[15] The facts of the novel, taken in and by themselves, are indeed the stuff of romantic and adventurous spectaculars; but what these facts signify is important if we hope to penetrate the "great Asian mystery."

On the simplest symbolic level, we find in this story the union between West and East represented by the love and by the assumed later marriage between Tancred and Eva. Disraeli employs this same symbolic formula in each of the three novels; aristocracy and trade have been joined in *Coningsby* (Coningsby and Edith), and the new Toryism and the people in *Sybil* (Egremont and Sybil). Now, as if to cap the regeneration, to make the new England complete, England is joined with the

East. By observing the order within this pyramid of marriages, we can see still another reason for *Tancred's* deviating from the political pattern set up by the two previous novels. The problem resolves itself to "first things first": there is a sequence of events which must take place if the new Toryism is to re-invigorate England.

First, the aristocracy must be realigned and solidified; the aristocracy of means (the Millbanks and the Traffords) must be taken in as equal partners by the aristocracy of birth (the Coningsbys and the Egremonts). The new Toryism is to be built upon a true aristocracy: those who either by birth or by wealth are in positions of authority and subscribe to the true tenets of the Tory ideal. Disraeli might easily ask what the differences are, except for the fact of birth, between a Millbank and a Trafford? Second, once the solidification and enunciation of authority have been made, there must take place a recognition on the part of authority that its primary duty is toward the masses of people dependent upon their "betters"; therefore, the concept of *noblesse oblige* must infuse the upper levels of the hierarchy. Thus the union between Egremont and Sybil emerges as symbolic of this second stage in the development of the Young England ideal.[16]

After this second stage, however, the political impasse is reached. Obviously, the ranks of the new aristocracy are not deep; the majority of aristocrats and factory owners are not receptive to the call of the new Toryism. Most remain "Buccaneers of Industry"; Carlyle's plea, which is in so many ways that of Young England also, falls upon unhearing, unyielding men. Since the Marneys, the Monmouths, and the Everinghams are still in control of the political scene, the third stage in the development of the Tory ideal must transcend the world of economics and politics. Indeed, this third stage in the sequence of events which will ultimately re-invigorate England must move to an area greater than politics and at the same time to one capable of giving real meaning and great principles to political parties and political action.

The meaning of the Asian mystery and the basis of that religious life which will orient political and social reorganization around great principles is to be found in the union of East and West. Just as Tancred sought to follow the route of his medieval ancestor, so Disraeli urges the West to seek its salvation in the East—by no means an easy task. We remember that Tancred was appalled when Lady Bertie and Bellair suggested a railroad from London to Jerusalem. Lady Bertie was distressed because of her young friend's forthcoming departure and Tancred suggested, therefore, that they all could go:

"That can never be," said Lady Bertie; "Augustus will never hear of it; he never could be absent more than six weeks from London, he misses his clubs so. If Jerusalem were only a place one could get at, something might be done; if there were a railroad to it for example."

"A railroad!" exclaimed Tancred, with a look of horror. "A railroad to Jerusalem!"

"No, I suppose there never can be one," continued Lady Bertie, in a musing tone. "There is no traffic." (*Tancred*, 167)

This exchange is telling as well as humorous. Just as mankind had attempted to reach heaven by building a tall tower at Babel, so Lady Bertie's obtuse, materialistic utilitarianism suggests the wrong way to reach Jerusalem. Symbolically, the railroad in this context represents the opposition view to the new Toryism; to Young England, it represents the wrong way to salvation— the expedient, Utilitarian view. It is thus a necessity that Tancred seek the basis for once more bringing great principles into English life, thereby implementing the unions symbolized in *Coningsby* and *Sybil*, and, in effect, solving the great "condition of England" question. That Augustus is unable to be away from the sterile though bustling life of his London clubs, that Tancred's England is in "an age of movement, but of confused ideas; a country of progress, but too rich to risk much change," and that "the spirit of the period and the people seeks a safety valve in bustle" so that "they do something, lest it be said that they do nothing" (*Tancred*, 75), all attest to the fact that England suffers from a disease which is corroding the very heart of the nation. Here in Disraelian terms we see presented Matthew Arnold's "furnace of the world" motif. There is no real plan or purpose to life. Man can push himself to work fifteen hours a day, do nothing, or do at most the same boring work each day—in no case is there happiness. The world so constituted "burns" man in any case; and, without aims and goals—great principles—there can be no success. For Young England, neither the moribund, old Toryism nor the soul-less, de-spiritualized Utilitarians offer such principles.

When Eva resumes the discussion of the Hebraeo-Christian concept begun by St. Lys, she prepares Tancred for entering into the Asian mystery. Upon waking from his sleep, Tancred speaks with Eva:

"This garden seems a paradise," said Tancred. "I had not thought that anything so fair could be found among these awful mountains. It is a spot that quite becomes Bethany."

"You Franks love Bethany?"

"Naturally; a place to us most dear and interesting."

"Pray, are you one of those Franks who worship a Jewess; or of those other who revile her, break her images, and blaspheme her pictures?"

"I venerate, though I do not adore, the mother of God," said Tancred, with emotion.

"Ah! the mother of Jesus!" said his companion. "He is your God. He lived much in this village. He was a great man, but he was a Jew; and you worship him."

"And you do not worship him?" said Tancred, looking up to her with an inquiring glance, and with a reddening cheek.

"It sometimes seems to me that I ought," said the lady, "for I am of his race, and you should sympathise with your race."

"You are, then a Hebrew?"

"I am of the same blood as Mary whom you venerate, but do not adore." (*Tancred*, 194-95)

Tancred tells Eva that she is "already half a Christian," to which she significantly responds: "But the Christianity which I draw from your book does not agree with the Christianity which you practise . . ." (*Tancred*, 195). She continues and enunciates the Hebrew origin of the Latin or Catholic Church and informs Tancred that "as for human agencies, we have a proverb: 'the will of man is the servant of God'" (*Tancred*, 198). Then, to underline the need of a union between West and East, Disraeli has Eva ask Tancred what is the most valued thing in Europe. Embarrassed, Tancred responds: "I think I know what ought to be most valued in Europe; it is something very different from what I fear I must confess is most valued there. My cheek burns while

I say it; but I think, in Europe, what is most valued is money"
(*Tancred,* 199).

Europe, in general, and England, in particular, Disraeli implies, respect and give honor to the wrong values. The right
values are to be found in the Hebrew faith and more readily
and easily in the amalgam of Hebraism and Christianity found
in the Primitive Church. This Primitive Church, in Disraeli's
view, was a direct outgrowth of Judaism and is therefore the
most significant depository of great Hebraeo-Christian principles.
All other churches build upon this one; but, through modifica-
tions of various sorts, they move farther and farther from the
essential truth of the church formed by the most direct apostolical succession possible, of the church at whose inception there
was a literal laying on of hands representing the two religions
which became one. (To be sure, there is also in Eva's speeches
a certain amount of pure propagandizing in behalf of the Jewish "race"—as Disraeli refers to it—but the core of her discussion
deals with the East-West question.)

Later in the novel Fakredeen proposes a scheme to Tancred
which not only foreshadows Disraeli's later political activities,
but which is most significant in the framework of the Asian
mystery. The Emir suggests that the East and the West be
joined through political combination, that the seat of the British
Empire be transplanted from London to Delhi, and that the
Queen of England become the Empress of India. The result of
such a combination must be the "greatest empire that ever ex-
isted" (*Tancred,* 270-71). Not only would it be a great empire,
but Disraeli implies it would be a *natural* empire. In this respect,
we should note Disraeli's comment on Tancred's journey—a comment which immediately follows Fakredeen's plan:

These Arabian laws regulated his [Tancred's] life. And the wander-
ings of an Arabian tribe in this "great and terrible wilderness," under
the immediate direction of the Creator, sanctified by His miracles,
governed by His counsels, illumined by His presence, had been the
first and guiding history that had been entrusted to his young intelligence, from which it had drawn its first pregnant examples of
human conduct and divine interposition, and formed its first dim
conceptions of the relations between man and God. Why, then, he
had a right to be here! He had a connection with these regions; they
had a hold upon him. He was not here like an Indian Brahmin, who

visits Europe from a principle of curiosity, however rational or however refined. The land which the Hindoo visits is not his land, nor his father's land; the laws which regulate it are not his laws, and the faith which fills its temples is not the revelation that floats upon his sacred Ganges. But for this English youth, words had been uttered and things done, more than thirty centuries ago, in this stony wilderness, which influenced his opinions and regulated his conduct every day of his life, in that distant and sea-girt home, which, at the time of their occurrence, was not as advanced in civilisation as the Polynesian groups or the islands of New Zealand. The life and property of England are protected by the laws of Sinai. (*Tancred*, 273)

This last sentence, then, in capsule form is the answer to the Asian mystery: "the life and property of England are protected by the laws of Sinai." By unmistakable implication, the Primitive Church, incorporating as it does the Mosaic and the Christian laws, affords the essential plan by which man can practically follow the teachings of Sinai brought to perfection, as it were, by Christ.[17] To recapitulate, Disraeli in *Coningsby* and *Sybil* offers his reading of the past in social and political terms; in *Tancred* he completes his secular trinity by invoking the past in religious terms.

The gap between the worlds of the flesh and of the spirit was great. That the gap must be bridged if the world of the flesh was to be saved was the uppermost thought in Tancred's mind:

The history of his [Tancred's] life and mind seemed with a whirling power to pass before him; his birth, in a clime unknown to the Patriarchs; his education, unconsciously to himself, in an Arabian literature; his imbibing, from his tender infancy, oriental ideas and oriental creeds; the contrast that the occidental society in which he had been reared presented to them; his dissatisfaction with that social system; his conviction of the growing melancholy of enlightened Europe, veiled, as it may be, with a sometimes conceited bustle, sometimes a desperate shipwreck gaiety, sometimes with all the exciting empiricism of science; his perplexity that, between the Asian revelation and the European practice, there should be so little conformity, and why the relations between them should be so limited and imperfect. . . . (*Tancred*, 278-79)

Fakredeen, who looks to Europe with envy for its trade, its money, and its power, comments upon Tancred's pilgrimage:

Society and Religion

"What can you want to do on Mount Sinai? Now if it were Mount Lebanon . . . there is an immense field. . . . We might establish manufactures, stimulate agriculture, extend commerce, get an appalto of the silk, buy it all up at sixty piastres per oke, and sell it at Marseilles at two hundred, and at the same time advance the interests of true religion as much as you please" (*Tancred*, 280). Disraeli brilliantly juxtaposes this speech almost directly after the above passage about Tancred, and in so doing clearly presents the English and European foil to Tancred's feelings.

Thus it is in *Tancred* that we are given the theoretical foundation of religious thought upon which men like Eustace Lyle in *Coningsby* and Aubrey St. Lys in *Sybil* can erect their practical applications of that religious medievalism. As Alfred North Whitehead observed, a society based upon Christian principles could not survive. We understand that neither Moses of the Old Testament nor Jesus of the New Testament had constructed in any operational form the societal, political, and religious institutions necessary to superstructure a complex social organism. However, Young England maintained that the great gift which the world received from "the God of Sinai and of Calvary" (to use Disraeli's term) was the ideological basis upon which the necessary secular institutions could be built. It was for the Primitive and the medieval Churches to translate the ideological message into practical terms, albeit always making certain that the final authority and the ultimate arbiter was the Law.

So it is in *Tancred* that Disraeli presents a devout, young man in conflict with his culture whose institutions had lost sight of the Law; and, therefore, he is a pilgrim in quest of the Law. Tancred's role is to enunciate once more the mystery of the God of Sinai and of Calvary in order that others may bring life into harmony with the Law. This is precisely, of course, the theory which underlies the Church of the Middle Ages. Once more in an age of growing skepticism, the search for authority is needed. Once more the spiritual nature of man must be re-affirmed. Once more in an age of utilitarian and material leveling of values, in a relativistic age of quantitative "push-pins," the hierarchical and qualitative "chain of being" must be re-established. So say the novel and Young England; and Disraeli, in *Tancred*, accomplishes these goals as Tancred probes the great Asian mystery.

Certainly the message which Tancred receives from the divine vision brings together the various concepts which fuse into the theoretical basis of Tancred's religious position:

"Child of Christendom," said the mighty form, as he seemed slowly to wave a sceptre fashioned like a palm tree. "I am the angel of Arabia, the guardian spirit of that land which governs the world; for power is neither the sword nor the shield, for these pass away, *but ideas which are divine. The thoughts of all lands come from a higher source than man,* but the intellect of Arabia comes from the Most High. Therefore it is that from this spot issue *the principles which regulate the human destiny.*

"That Christendom which thou has quitted, *and over whose expiring attributes thou art a mourner,* was a savage forest while the cedars of Lebanon, for countless ages, had built the palaces of mighty kings. Yet in that forest brooded infinite races that were to spread over the globe, and give a new impulse to its ancient life. It was deemed that, when they burst from their wild woods, the Arabian principles should meet them on the threshold of the old world to guide and to civilise them. All had been prepared. The Caesars had conquered the world to place the Laws of Sinai on the throne of the Capitol, and a Galilean Arab advanced and traced on the front of the rude conquerors of the Caesars the subduing symbol of the last development of Arabian principles.

"*Yet again, and Europe is in the throes of a great birth.* The multitudes again are brooding; but they are not now in the forests; they are in the cities and in the fertile plains. . . . Now they despair. But the eternal principles that controlled barbarian vigour can alone cope with morbid civilisation. *The equality of man can only be accomplished by the sovereignty of God. The longing for fraternity can never be satisfied but under the sway of a common father.* The relations between Jehovah and his creatures can be neither too numerous nor too near. In the increased distance between God and man have grown up all these developments that have made life mournful. *Cease, then, to seek in a vain philosophy the solution of the social problem that perplexes you. Announce the sublime and solacing doctrine of theocratic equality.* Fear not, faint not, falter not. *Obey the impulse of thine own spirit, and find a ready instrument in every human being.*" (*Tancred,* 299-300 [italics mine])

In addition to the previously stated terms of the ideological message of the God of Sinai and of Calvary, this speech reiterates

certain of Disraeli's favorite themes which we have already
met in other works. The most striking motif of the angel's
message is the reworking of the phoenix image (which Carlyle
developed in "Organic Filaments"). Europe is at present in
a state of expiration, at which death Tancred is a mourner;
but, at the same time, the angel declares that "Europe is in
the throes of a great birth." Out of this death of a mock, Euro-
pean-style Christendom will rise the true concepts of Hebraeo-
Christian Law. Indeed, invoking Carlyle once again, do we
not perceive in the angel's speech an explicit notion of organic
filaments, and, still further, of the Kantian distinction (so popular
with Carlyle and Disraeli) between the realms of phenomena
and noumena?

In addition, the figure of the hero in Carlylean-Disraelian terms
emerges in the person of Tancred. That there are two worlds,
one transcending the other, is apparent in the angel's statement
that "the thoughts of all lands come from a higher source than
man. . . ." The principles by which man's life and destiny must
be regulated are not to be gleaned from the world of phenomena.
These true principles can be learned only by piercing through
the world of phenomena into the world of noumena and thus
coming into tune with the organic filaments, those ideas by which
society can be rewoven. Ideas are divine, says the angel, as he
urges Tancred on in his mission. Tancred is the hero; he looks
more deeply into things and refuses to be misled by shams (for
example, his refusal to enter Parliament). The angel charges him
to announce the Law, obey his own spirit, and convert those
who must be bound to the world of phenomena.

The angel (directed as he is by Disraeli) strongly implies the
hierarchical structure of worldly society by announcing that
"theocratic equality" is the only equality; men are equal only
in the sight of God. Since man's equality and "fraternity" can
be brought about only by God, the angel urges the West to
cease seeking in a "vain philosophy," a term which must be
interpreted broadly. The "vain philosophy" on one level is obviously the ideology of the Utilitarians, but on a more encompass-
ing one it is the entire philosophy of materialistic and mercenary
expediency out of which Young England saw Utilitarianism grow,
an expediency which in its growth necessarily destroyed the

Church's spiritual functions. In its simplest terms, the angel's speech announces that the East (the realm of noumena) and the West (the realm of phenomena) must unite to produce the birth of the new phoenix.

As if to illustrate the theme of the novel, Disraeli offers as a leitmotif the history of the Baroni family. In this family we see in microcosmic view the Hebraeo-Christian concept, the blending of East and West which is in essence the answer to the riddle of the Asian mystery. From a life of relative obscurity as a group of itinerant entertainers, the Baroni family is given by Sidonia the opportunity to show its genius. Twenty years after Sidonia met the family, its fame was everywhere known:

Mademoiselle Josephine is at this moment the glory of the French stage; without any question the most admirable tragic actress since Clairon, and inferior not even to her. The spirit of French tragedy has risen from the imperial couch on which it had long slumbered since her appearance, at the same time classical and impassioned, at once charmed and commanded the most refined audience in Europe. Adele, under the name of Madame Baroni, is the acknowledged Queen of Song in London, Paris, Berlin, and St. Petersburg; while her younger sister, Carlotta Baroni, shares the triumphs, and equals the renown of a Taglioni and a Cerito. At this moment, Madame Baroni performs to enthusiastic audiences in the first opera of her brother Michel, who promises to be the rival of Meyerbeer and Mendelssohn; all delightful intelligence to meet the ear of the soft-hearted Alfred, who is painting the new chambers of the Papal palace, a Cavaliere, decorated with many orders, and the restorer of the once famous Roman school. (*Tancred*, 345-46)

Tancred, utterly amazed at this incredible performance of a single family, ponders the question of how this one family came from obscurity to disseminate its genius throughout the world, charming mankind in the process. The answer to this "mystery" lies in two facts. First, it was fortunate for the Baroni group that Sidonia "had so much feeling for genius." Second, the Baroni family needed but the opportunity of discovery since it had the necessary genius. In Disraelian terms, the Baronis had the genius of race: the family has the touch of genius produced by the Hebraeo-Christian complex, by the union of East and West. Their name suggests a Roman Catholic ethnic background, Italian or

Spanish. Yet their religion is Hebrew. The very blending which lay at the heart of the Asian mystery is seen in this family—the apostolical succession in terms of ethnic, national, and religious commingling. Indeed, the elder Baroni indicates the union when he tells Tancred, in discussing the name Baroni: "the name of old clothes men in London, and of caliphs at Baghdad" (*Tancred*, 346). In allegorical terms, then, Tancred is to Sidonia as the Asian mystery is to the Baroni family. Tancred has the feelings for genius in spiritual terms—thus his pilgrimage to the East. The genius of the Law of the God of Sinai and of Calvary exists only to be re-discovered and disseminated throughout the world to "charm" all mankind.

In more precise terms, Disraeli ties the theme of *Tancred* to those of *Coningsby* and *Sybil* by discussing a movement in the East called the Young Syrian movement: "It flourishes: in every town and village of Lebanon, there is a band of youth who acknowledge the title, and who profess nationality as their object, though, behind that plea, the restoration of the house of Shehaab generally peeps out" (*Tancred*, 359). What is most significant about the goal of Young Syria is the dominant characteristic of the house of Shehaab: feudalism. Young Syria feared the abolition of the hierarchical social structure under which its people had lived, prospered, and were happy: "The peril in which feudalism was placed revived their ancient sentiments" (*Tancred*, 359). The most striking statement of the East's goals is made by Tancred himself: "We wish to conquer that world, with angels at our head, in order that we may establish the happiness of man by a divine dominion, and, crushing the political atheism that is now desolating existence, utterly extinguish the grovelling tyranny of self-government" (*Tancred*, 434). Thus Disraeli manages in this novel to make the full swing back to the essential aims of his Young England followers and to the political and social views of *Coningsby* and *Sybil*. The hierarchical societal pattern, the heroic aristocracy recognizing its true responsibilities,[18] the harmonious nature of existence, the spiritual dignity and nobility of the individual man, the creative rendering of the Kantian distinction—all the major motifs of the previous two novels are found in *Tancred*.

Overriding all of these concepts is the ultimate purpose of the novel: the exploration of the meaning of the great Asian mystery. In order for the myriad social and political goals to be made effectively and lastingly operational, they and the culture for which they are meant must be based upon the authority of the primitive Hebraeo-Christian Church.[19] Ultimately, the Law of the God of Sinai and of Calvary must be the source for all other laws, just as the dynamo of the medieval synthesis must be the source of the organic filaments. From the Church and religion, the social and political institutions of life must gain their strength, wisdom, and direction.

CHAPTER 6

Last Novels:
Lothair *and* Endymion

D URING the last eleven years of his life, Disraeli wrote two
novels and began a third which remained unfinished at
his death. Many years had passed and much had happened to
and around Disraeli between the completion of *Tancred* in 1847
and the publication of *Lothair* in 1870. The fact that thirty-three
years elapsed between two novels by the same novelist must
be considered one of the curiosities of English literary history.
Indeed, the arrival of Disraeli's last novel, *Endymion,* in 1880
was in fact more than fifty years after the publication of his
first, *Vivian Grey,* in 1826. This tremendous span of time
prompted Lord Derby to say at the publication of *Endymion*
that "there were three remarkable things about it, (1) he knew
no other novel in English written by a man of 75, or (2) published 50 years after a former novel by the same author, or (3)
written by a man after he had been Prime Minister (except, of
course, *Lothair*)."[1]
All that Derby said is true, but the most significant comment
remained unsaid. The author of *Lothair* and *Endymion* is not
only an older man, but he is also a considerably different man
from the author of the Young England trilogy. These last
novels constitute the third phase of Disraeli's literary career.
Just as we have seen significant differences between the early
novels and the trilogy, so we can readily perceive a new point
of view and outlook in the last works. No longer are we in the
presence of a dandified, autobiographical, "silver-fork" novelist
or of an ideological crusader. Instead, we now meet with an
old, tired, partially disappointed but always acute observer of
politics and society.

By 1870 Benjamin Disraeli was an elder statesman and a parliamentary hero. Two years earlier, Queen Victoria had offered him a peerage; but to leave his greatest battleground, the House of Commons, was too great a price to pay for a title. The great statesman was not yet ready to give up active politics. Often in his novels we are told that an MP's greatest love is Parliament and that the most precious gift England can bestow upon a subject is election to it. Disraeli lived this sentiment; but in 1869 the Whigs were in power, Disraeli was in opposition, and there was time to work on the novel he had been contemplating for some time. The following year saw the publication of *Lothair*; and, after months of enormous sales, there could be no doubt of the popularity of the author.

I   Lothair (1870)

For the chronologically oriented reader who has just completed the trilogy, *Lothair* presents certain immediate problems. Disraeli here demonstrates a new point of view, for he is now more an observer and less a crusader. He more closely approaches, therefore, that paradoxical involved detachment of the writer. *Lothair* is a political novel without an ideology to be imaginatively presented, for it is based upon "a desire to mirror and satirise the passing show."[2] The plot is more complex, fortunately, than its central character who is a rather simple, untutored creature buffeted by circumstances. Things happen to Lothair, and he has kinship with the world of literary characters of the cut of Nicholas Nickleby—we might perhaps call it the "Nickleby Syndrome"—who are moved by the plot without ever once returning the favor.

Our hero has lost his heart several times during the course of the novel, and it is perhaps fitting that he finally marries the least interesting and exciting of the females who cross his path. Yet the marriage to Lady Corisande is the necessary one in the figurative terms of the novel's higher meaning: Lothair rejects both Roman Catholicism and the common-law religion of the secret societies in order to embrace the Anglican tradition. We wonder, however, whether Disraeli wholly approved of Lothair's decision; and we should bear in mind that of the three women with whom Lothair was most taken, only Lady Corisande was ultimately available for marriage. The already married Theodora hád 'died, and Clare Arundel had finally made her decision to enter the veiled sisterhood of the Catholic Church. The novel makes it manifestly clear that if Theodora had been in a position to marry Lothair, the marriage would have taken place. How the book then might have moved remains an interesting question. Perhaps the problem of ultimate meaning in this novel can best be resolved by considering the three positions representatively held by Lothair's three loves.

Although Theodora is the most striking and dramatic of the women, her ideological position is not only the least tenable but certainly the most repugnant to Disraeli himself. She is at the heart of the Continental secret societies which breed revolution and which defy tradition and the concept of property. Her ultimate goal is some sort of egalitarian, socio-political structure freed from the bonds of traditional religion, statecraft, and economics. For this rather nebulous, loosely defined idea, Theodora is willing to and indeed does sacrifice her life. That her movement is crushed by its most intense enemy, the Catholic Church, does little to negate the ideology of her position, just as it does nothing to elevate the ideology of the victorious Holy See.

However, the defeat of Theodora—engineered as it is, of course, by the author—probably indicates the value judgment of the novelist. It is clear from Disraeli's life and works that he would be unfavorably disposed to most of the secret societies' positions. The political position, in particular, would obviously clash with Disraeli's reliance (at least in an ideological sense) on the past and tradition. Furthermore, we must assume that somewhere between the religious position outlined in the Young England trilogy and the Anglican Church, we find Disraeli's own religious beliefs. Although I feel they are closer to that religion of the trilogy than to that of the Church of England, it is, nevertheless, obvious that Disraeli's position runs counter to that of Theodora and her followers. We know, of course, relatively little concerning Disraeli's personal beliefs. About religion, as about most other private matters, the Prime Minister was silent. For this reason alone the novels judiciously read take on considerable biographical importance although we must always bear in mind Waldershare's comment in *Endymion*:

"As for that," said Waldershare, "sensible men are all of the same religion."
"And pray what is that?" inquired the prince.
"Sensible men never tell." (371)

Although the Roman Catholic Church formed one half of the Hebraeo-Christian synthesis which lies at the heart of *Tancred*, the Catholic Church is treated in *Lothair* as harshly as Theodora's secret societies. Thoroughly despicable practices of contemporary Church fathers are laid bare by Disraeli's narrator; and, through Lothair's complex entanglements with Rome, a less than flattering picture of the Church emerges. However, there are significant and necessary qualifications which we must make when attempting to assess and understand Disraeli's handling of the Church in *Lothair*. These qualifications indicate that the distance between the treatment of Roman Catholicism in *Lothair* and that of the Hebraeo-Christian synthesis in the trilogy, especially in *Tancred*, is not so great as may first appear.

The target of Disraeli's attack in *Lothair* is the Catholic hierarchy and the influential lay individuals rather than the Catholic Church as an historical entity. This point is made even more significant when we consider the target within the secret societies. Theodora is presented most sympathetically as are her husband and the general; indeed, they are often treated as exemplary human beings. The ideological commitment which motivates them, on the other hand, is scorned by the novelist. Thus Disraeli is able to attack the policies of the secret societies but at the same time to find merit in some of the practitioners. In the treatment of the Roman Church, we find the reverse situation present; for Disraeli makes a distinction between the Catholic continuum and the contemporary practitioners of that historical movement. With the exception of Clare Arundel, the Catholic member of Lothair's trio of loves, it is upon the practitioners that Disraeli's ire falls. Surely Disraeli would find it difficult indeed to reject altogether so considerable an element of his earlier works. Furthermore, the treatment of this same subject in *Endymion* is distinctly different from the handling of

Catholics in *Lothair*. As we shall see in Disraeli's last complete novel, the Church is once more viewed in a sympathetic manner.

Lady Corisande, who ultimately becomes Lothair's wife, is the rather bland representative of the Anglican Church whose primary function in this novel is to maintain a posture of shocked dismay as the Catholic Church entices Church of England men to her Roman bosom. That Corisande emerges victorious over both Theodora and Clare is more significant in terms of Disraeli's desire that the Anglican Church prevail than in terms of Corisande's involvement in the plot. Yet to suggest that these three women represent the only possible commitments which the novel offers is to omit both Mr. Phoebus and the mystical Paraclete, both of whom offer other possibilities. We sometimes wonder if Disraeli is here sorting out the five alternate ideological commitments that he has witnessed during the past fifty years.

The overriding critical problem in *Lothair* involves the question of Disraeli's voice in the novel, as for example, in the speech of the Cardinal:

"I know not a grander or a nobler career for a young man of talents and position in this age, than to be the champion and asserter of Divine truth. It is not probable that there could be another conqueror in our time. The world is wearied of statesmen, whom democracy has degraded into politicians, and of orators who have become what they call debaters. I do not believe there could be another Dante, even another Milton. The world is devoted to physical science, because it believes these discoveries will increase its capacity of luxury and self-indulgence. But the pursuit of science leads only to the insoluble. When we arrive at that barren term, the Divine voice summons man, as it summoned Samuel; all the poetry and passion and sentiment of human nature are taking refuge in religion; and he whose deeds and words most nobly represent Divine thoughts, will be the man of this century." (67)

The Cardinal's comments might very well be Disraeli's. Although the position advanced by the Catholic Church in *Lothair* is rejected, much that is said in behalf of the Church and of tradition is within the Young England frame of reference, all of which had certainly not left Disraeli's sensibilities. We must remember also that Disraeli understood full well the popular interest in the subject of young nobles going over to Rome, and he also recognized the deep English resentment and distrust of the Church. He was in one sense, then, capitalizing on popular topics. But to read the novel's view of Roman Catholicism in isolation (outside of the context shaped by both Disraeli's own life and thought) is to misread Disraeli's full view of the Roman Catholic Church. We must also bear in mind that the very first anti-Catholic remark in a Disraeli novel is in *Venetia* (78), and neither is it significant nor is it spoken by a significant character.[3] Similarly, even though there are a few veiled assaults on Roman Catholicism in the Young England trilogy, those novels finally underscore the ethos of the Church. The point is that it is impossible to accept the view of the Roman Catholic Church found in *Lothair* as Disraeli's final or most mature view of the subject.

In the years between *Tancred* in 1847 and *Lothair* in 1870, the facts of life had become very real for Disraeli. He had come some distance from the days of Young England and must have clearly understood by 1870 the impossibilities inherent in the tentative movements of the enthusiastic young men who had surrounded him so many years before. In Lothair's ever increasing realization of the complexities of life we find one key to Disraeli's later view. Early in the novel Lothair announces that his "opinions are already formed on every subject . . . of importance; and, what is more, they will never change" (15). At this moment of smugly confident youth, Lothair is certain of his reading of life and society. The novel's plot, however, not only overturns Lothair's views, but brings him to a realization of the complexities of dealing with the greater questions of society, religion, and education. It takes but a short time for Lothair to understand that his original opinions will not carry him far: "It [that time of certainty] seems like a dream; but everything seems like a dream: I hardly know whether life is agony or bliss" (77). Also early in the novel the narrator describes General Bruges' effect upon the Standing Committee of the Holy Alliance of Peoples who "all rose, although they were extreme Republicans, when the General entered. Such is the magical influence of a man of action over men of the pen and the tongue" (44). Late in the novel the General offers advice to Lothair:

"Whatever you do," said the General, "give up dreams."
"I think you may be right in that," said Lothair, with half a sigh.

"Action may not always be happiness," said the General; "but there is no happiness without action. If you will not fight the Egyptians, were I you, I would return home and plunge into affairs. That was a fine castle of yours I visited one morning; a man who lives in such a place must be able to find a great deal to do." (407)

We must ask whether Bruges' advice to Lothair is the advice that the Disraeli of 1870 would have offered to Tancred and to the men of Young England: action instead of dreams. Is Disraeli now more sympathetic to Baron Fleming than to Contarini? We do not know, for counterpointed against this refrain of action in the midst of a complex world is another melody which brings back the strains of the Young England novels: the conception of the hero.

At about the same time that General Bruges is greeted by the Standing Committee, the Cardinal interviews Lothair. The Cardinal's conversation revolves around the heroic possibilities inherent in Lothair: ". . . I perceive in you great qualities . . . that . . . may considerably affect the history of this country, and perhaps even a wider range" (69). In the churchman's view, Lothair has the "necessary gifts" including "implicit faith in the Divine purpose." Lothair is as captivated and excited after this meeting with the Cardinal as Coningsby and Egremont had been after their meetings with Sidonia and Gerard: "Lothair returned to town excited and agitated. He felt that he was on the eve of some great event in his existence, but its precise character was not defined" (70). He meditates on the nature of the hero in terms much like those articulated by Young England: "Human beings who had been in personal relation with the Godhead must be different from other human beings. There must be some transcendent quality in their lives and careers, in their very organisation, which marks them out from all secular heroes" (71). In retrospect, however, the reader is aware that this is a discordant contrapuntal movement since Lothair obviously does not emerge as heroic.

We can perhaps explain Lothair's non-heroic state in two ways. First, the church surrogates' motives are neither genuine nor sincere. Second, Disraeli had certainly realized long before 1870 that political progress and social amelioration are not achieved through commitment to abstract principle alone. Coningsby and Egremont were no doubt seen as more pragmatically correct than Tancred, although Tancred's conclusions might still stand as theoretically sound. Disraeli has seen too much of the real and inside world of social and political power to still cling to the romantic credo of Young England. Although that former movement might remain enticing, even captivating, there was little likelihood of a heroic person's successfully manifesting himself in nineteenth-century British life and government. Thus in *Lothair*, although many of the external characteristics of the hero are present in both plot and theme, they are invariably blasted by the facts of life in the world of this novel, a world closer to the real than that reflected in the Young England novels. Again, however, the question of Disraeli's voice in *Lothair* obtrudes. Even though there is little question concerning the novel's final assessment of the heroic motif, the matter is complicated by the introduction of Paraclete. After having articulated the positions represented by Theodora, Clare, and Corisande, Disraeli moves Mr. Phoebus and then Paraclete to the center of the novel's stage.

The reader does not take Mr. Phoebus seriously until rather late in the novel. His most stunning early appearance has him in the garb of a quasi-eugenist who addresses himself to the "condition of England" question from an uncommon as well as untenable perspective. Starting from the perfectly respectable position that the first duty of the state is "to attend to the frame and health of the subject," Phoebus moves to his reading of Spartan planned parenthood which will produce an Aryan race of superior beings; and not even the still impressionable Lothair can accept this solution. So Mr. Phoebus drops from sight for some two hundred pages until he returns to aid Lothair after his escape from his Catholic abductors. At this point Phoebus presents what we might consider the novel's fourth possible commitment: a selfish devotion to sensory gratification. The Phoebus party is interested in pleasure, the cultivation of what it calls *taste*; and its conception of true religion is the worship of the beautiful. Only by overly ingenious exegesis could the reader detect Disraeli's voice in Mr. Phoebus' pronouncements, but Phoebus acts as a foil to Paraclete in whose views there is a good deal of the Young England Disraeli.

The introduction of Paraclete into this novel is in one sense anachronistic: a Sidonia-like counsellor, he invokes traditional religious views, the East, the Hebrew race, and the conception of Christianity as completed Judaism. Furthermore, when Lothair says, "I wish to visit the cradle of my faith," he sounds strikingly like Tancred. And Paraclete, whose name itself is symbolic of his function, responds with a line right out of the *milieu* of *Tancred*: "And you would do wisely . . . for there is no doubt the spiritual nature of man is developed in this land" (394). That Paraclete is given the last act of the novel raises meaningful questions concerning the nature of Disraeli's real commitments in 1870. Clearly not the same as those articulated in the 1840's, they are by no means antithetical to the Young England ethos—an important point for any student of Disraeli.

By and large, the usual approach to the last novels has been an historical one: readers have generally examined *Lothair* and *Endymion* for Disraeli's reading of English political and social history from roughly 1830. Without doubt, this approach in itself is legitimate; the point here, however, is that such a reading does not go far enough; for it overlooks the ideational, perhaps ideological, complexities present. As has been already suggested, the last novels are different in kind as well as in motivation from the Young England trilogy, just as Disraeli himself has changed over those years.[4] Thus the *emphasis* of Disraeli's last works is different from the trilogy without, however, ignoring several of the considerable subjects treated in the author's most significant novels.

Once more, then, we come back to the problem of the author's voice in *Lothair*. Just as we have seen Disraeli's sensibilities operating in a speech made by the Cardinal, so we find the same situation present in almost every remark made by Paraclete. In the following passage, for example, Paraclete is responding to Lothair's concern that scientific investigation has reduced individual man to a position of insignificance.

Science may prove the insignificance of this globe in the scale of creation . . . but it cannot prove the insignificance of man. What is the earth compared with the sun? a molehill by a mountain; yet the inhabitants of this earth can discover the elements of which the great orb consists, and will probably ere long ascertain all the conditions of its being. Nay, the human mind can penetrate far beyond the sun. There is no relation therefore between the faculties of man and the scale in creation of the planet which he inhabits. (394)

Finally, of course, we must ask which voice is indeed the author's, and the answer is not a simple one.

Yet I would suggest that Disraeli has more sympathy with the Cardinal's abstract sentiments than with his practical plans, with Theodora's desire to elevate the condition of the masses than with her means for achieving her goals, with Corisande's reliance on the instrumentality of the Anglican Church than with her passive defense of that church, with Mr. Phoebus' notions of taste and beauty than with his bizarre plans for implementing them, with Paraclete's theoretical pronouncements than with his unconcern for the pragmatic means by which they could be brought to pass. The point is that there is no one voice in *Lothair* which can be singled out as belonging to the author, but there are many moments in the novel at which we can clearly detect Disraeli's temporary incarnation in one of his character's forms. It is through the process of collecting those moments at which the author's voice is heard that the reader comes to realize that although there is a considerable intellectual and ideological distance between *Tancred* and *Lothair*, many of the earlier novel's motifs are rehearsed in the later novel. By virtue of their placement in a position secondary to politics and social history, however, the reader is aware of the author's growth since the earlier novel. Disraeli's mind in 1870 is still captivated by some aspects of the Young England program, merely titillated by others, and realistically aware of the impossibility of much of the former movement's credo.

II Endymion (1880)

The plot skeleton of *Endymion* concerns the fortunes of the Ferrars family. Endymion and Myra Ferrars, twins, are born into a family soon to face misfortune. After having spent their early years living in luxurious ease and having been prepared to become haughty and insufferably "superior" adults, the brother and sister are reduced to the disenchanted world of poverty by the fall from power of their father's political party. The gay, sparkling, and expensive London life was reluctantly traded for a quiet, rustic, and inexpensive provincial existence. The elder Ferrars, who might have been Prime Minister had the Whigs remained in power, gave himself to political writing, while his wife who had been dedicated to the world of fashionable society awaited her husband's return to political power. Although the call never came, the children managed to survive hopefully and reasonably happily only because they were with each other. The bond between them was great, and early in their lives Myra had pledged her life to the cause of her brother's future.

Events became more dismal for the Ferrars family. The Whigs returned to power, but old Ferrars, who had been away from the political center, London, for too long a time, was not offered a substantial place in the new government. The children were separated when Endymion was sent to London to work as a minor clerk in the Treasury. Soon after Mrs. Ferrars' death, Mr. Ferrars committed suicide, leaving his children penniless. But from this point on, the twins' fortunes increase in so spectacular and grand a fashion that by the end of the novel Endymion is Prime Minister of England, and Myra is the Queen of a great European state. The events of this change in the family situation—engineered essentially by Myra—constitute the body of the novel.

It has been suggested by some readers and by Disraeli himself that the primary purpose of *Endymion* was to indicate the power of women in the careers of men. This motif appears in most Disraeli novels, and its culmination is certainly present in *Endymion*. Almost as though Disraeli were returning the favor to the many women who had been instrumental in guiding his literary and political careers, the former Prime Minister creates the character and fortunes of Endymion Ferrars. It is primarily through the aid of the "softer sex" that the protagonist is moved from insignificant clerk in an undistinguished government bureau to Prime Minister. On this level, the novel is not only a fairy tale but it suffers from the suspension of disbelief which readers must bring with them to fairy tales. In any final analysis, Endymion Ferrars is an unimpressive young man whose most cherished commitment is freedom from commitment. The "middle way" is Endymion's hallmark. He desires never to be the instrument which fractures other men's ideas, views, or alliances. He is, in a word, another insipid protagonist. Nevertheless, *Endymion* is a meaningful novel, and it is obviously another level of interest to which we must move in order to harvest any more fruitful reading than that offered by the plot fortunes of the Ferrars.

Remembering that this novel was written by a man just retired permanently from politics (Gladstone and the Liberals had just defeated the seventy-six-year-old Disraeli and his Conservatives) and bearing also in mind that Disraeli was at the end of a very long and full career as a public figure, we can read *Endymion* as the imaginative recollections of its author; indeed, *Endymion* is that more than anything else. Through this book the years from 1827 to the late 1850's once more come to life—always, however, with Disraeli operating as the life-giver. By using as the stuff of his novel the actual events and the "real" people of that era, Disraeli can re-create and sometimes create the years of his coming of age. In the Young England trilogy we have seen the great political backdrop employed by the author, but nowhere in Disraeli's works is the political and social history of nineteenth-century England so pervasive a character as in *Endymion*. In Disraeli's novels generally the political scene functions as a character—in many ways, it is the most dynamic, round character in the works. In *Endymion*, as in life itself, the fates of the central figures are at least partially shaped by politics.

As in *Lothair*, Disraeli's treatment of politics and society is different from what it had been in the trilogy. As in *Lothair*, the author observes, sometimes passes overt judgment; but he almost always comments through his tone. At his best, Disraeli is a brilliant satirist; and in *Endymion* in particular the satirist becomes manifestly plain. Although Disraeli's aphoristic skill has been often and justly pointed out, his ability to engage the reader's attention in sustained satire is an even more striking accomplishment. So sustained can his satire become that the reader may almost forget the tone and can—if he is not careful —extract the wrong meaning from the letter of the word.[5] The handling of the railroad mania which swept across England

in the 1840's is such an example in *Endymion*. Disraeli treats the
subject at some length and from a variety of vantage points:
Endymion, Mr. Vigo, Parliament, and the people. But transcending the humor and satire of the novel are the love—often un-
abashed—which Disraeli demonstrates for an age gone by and
the devotion which he shows to politics.

The novel opens with a dialogue which announces one of the
great themes of nineteenth-century life: change and transition.
Significantly counterpointed against Sidney Wilton's realization
of his age's change is the older Ferrars' insistence that all needed
change has already occurred—and this statement is made in 1827:

"Well," said his companion [Sidney Wilton] musingly, "it may be
fancy, but I cannot resist the feeling that this country, and the world
generally, are on the eve of a great change—and I do not think the
Duke is the man for the epoch."

"I see no reason why there should be any great change; certainly
not in this country," said Mr. Ferrars. "Here we have changed everything that was required. Peel has settled the criminal law, and Huskisson the currency, and though I am prepared myself still further to
reduce the duties on foreign imports, no one can deny that on this
subject the Government is in advance of public opinion."

"The whole affair rests on too contracted a basis," said his companion. "We are habituated to its exclusiveness, and, no doubt,
custom in England is a power; but let some event suddenly occur
which makes a nation feel or think, and the whole thing might vanish
like a dream."

"What can happen? Such affairs as the Luddites do not occur twice
in a century, and as for Spafields riots, they are impossible now with
Peel's new police. The country is employed and prosperous, and were
it not so, the landed interest would always keep things straight."

"It is powerful, and has been powerful for a long time; but there
are other interests besides the landed interest now."

"Well, there is the colonial interest, and the shipping interest,"
said Mr. Ferrars, "and both of them thoroughly with us."

"I was not thinking of them," said his companion. "It is the
increase in population, and of a population not employed in the
cultivation of the soil, and all the consequences of such circumstances
that were passing over my mind." (3-4)

Thus on the first pages of the novel Disraeli introduces the major
motif of his last complete work. The book's most powerful chap-

ters deal with the political and social change which Disraeli describes expertly. From his brief but incisive assessment of the Duke of Wellington and his government—"The government of the Duke could only be measured by his life, and his influence was irresistible. It was a dictatorship of patriotism. The country, long accustomed to a strong and undisturbed administration, and frightened by the changes and catastrophes which had followed the retirement of Lord Liverpool, took refuge in the powerful will and splendid reputation of a real hero" (21) —Disraeli moves to an account of the state of English society in 1829 and 1830, an account which is in reality a brief, brilliant essay in comparative society (1829-30 contrasted, often by implication, with the 1870's):

The great world then, compared with the huge society of the present period, was limited in its proportions, and composed of elements more refined though far less various. It consisted mainly of the great landed aristocracy, who had quite absorbed the nabobs of India, and had nearly appropriated the huge West Indian fortunes. Occasionally, an eminent banker or merchant invested a large portion of his accumulations in land, and in the purchase of parliamentary influence, and was in time duly admitted into the sanctuary. But those vast and successful invasions of society by new classes which have since occurred, though impending, had not yet commenced. The manufacturers, the railway kings, the colossal contractors, the discoverers of nuggets, had not yet found their place in society and the senate. There were then, perhaps, more great houses open than at the present day, but there were very few little ones. The necessity of providing regular occasions for the assembling of the miscellaneous world of fashion led to the institution of Almack's, which died out in the advent of the new system of society, and in the fierce competition of its inexhaustible private entertainments.

The season then was brilliant and sustained, but it was not flurried. People did not go to various parties on the same night. They remained where they were assembled, and, not being in a hurry, were more agreeable than they are at the present day. Conversation was more cultivated; manners, though unconstrained, were more stately; and the world, being limited, knew itself much better. On the other hand, the sympathies of society were more contracted than they are at present. The pressure of population had not opened the heart of man. The world attended to its poor in its country parishes, and subscribed and danced for the Spitalfields weavers when their normal distress had overflowed, but their knowledge of the people did not exceed these bounds, and the people knew very little more about themselves. They were only half born.

The darkest hour precedes the dawn, and a period of unusual stillness often, perhaps usually, heralds the social convulsion. At this moment the general tranquillity and even content were remarkable. In politics the Whigs were quite prepared to extend to the Duke the same provisional confidence that had been accepted by Mr. Canning, and conciliation began to be an accepted phrase, which meant in practice some share on their part of the good things of the State. The country itself required nothing. There was a general impression, indeed, that they had been advancing at a rather rapid rate, and that it was as well that the reins should be entrusted to a wary driver. (22-23)

The novel is filled with such virtuoso pieces: the changes taking place in politics and society in the years 1832-35 (69-70), the 1834-35 general elections (71-73), London in the 1830's (82), the political situation of 1838-39 (239-40), the Montfort Tournament (253-67), and the condition of England in 1842 (349-57) are only several examples. As Philip Guedalla has suggested, "a full commentary on *Endymion* would make a passable history of England from 1827 to 1855."[6] But, in addition to the historical quality of the work, there are several features of Disraeli's thought in this novel which are particularly meaningful in the light of my previous discussion.

I have already suggested that the apparent treatment of Roman Catholicism in *Lothair* is contradicted not only by Disraeli's thought and works prior to 1870 but also by his last novel in which the subject is once again sympathetically treated. If there is any question about Disraeli's debt to the past, to tradition, and to the Hebraeo-Christian synthesis of the Young England novels, a close reading of *Endymion* should answer it. In this novel the author responds to his life-long commitment to tradition, and he does so in a variety of terms. It is Waldershare, late in the novel, who bluntly attacks the claim that liberal and Roman Catholic are polar terms: "Old fashioned twaddle of the Liberal party. . . . There is more true democracy in the Roman Catholic Church than in all the secret societies of Europe" (370). Obviously, we must ask how meaningful this view is in terms of Disraeli's own thinking on the subject. Waldershare is, after all, based upon George Smythe of the old Young England days. Is this view, then, an ironic throwback to those earnest young men of the forties? Is it something Disraeli still believes? Does it really counteract the view seemingly presented in *Lothair*? Is the statement merely a comment on the limitations of Waldershare? To answer these questions, we must view the novel's entire approach to Roman Catholicism. If the Waldershare remark were the only overt Catholic reference in the novel, we would have to dismiss it in terms of thematic significance. However, it is, in fact, surrounded by a variety of Catholic plot elements and references. Thus not only is Waldershare's comment meaningful, but Disraeli's final literary response to the subject in itself and to the much larger topic of traditional principles can be seen clearly in the novel.

One key to reading the novel's view of Catholicism lies in the character of Nigel Penruddock. In Nigel's movement from son of a rural Anglican rector to Papal Legate and Archbishop, Disraeli mirrors not only the kind of spiritual odyssey undertaken by many nineteenth-century Anglicans, but in his treatment of Nigel he undercuts the depiction of Catholic prelates in *Lothair*. Further and perhaps most meaningful in terms of Disraeli's continued interest in tradition are Nigel's reasons for moving to the Roman Church. From his earliest moments in the novel, Nigel is dedicated to a conception of natural law and to the great principles which recall to the reader the credo of Young England. Tancred would agree with Nigel's comment that the Church "was founded by God; all other governments have been founded by men. When they are destroyed, and the process of destruction seems rapid, there will be nothing left to govern mankind except the Church" (54). This is a young, Anglican, university student speaking—one who in the 1840's would probably have rushed into the Young England fold. Instead, he enters the Catholic Church; but he sounds almost always like theologized Coningsbys, Egremonts, and Tancreds:

"I know nothing about Whigs or Tories or Liberals, or any other new names which they invent. . . . Nor do I know, or care to know, what Low Church means. There is but one Church, and it is catholic and apostolic; and if we act on its principles, there will be no need, and there ought to be no need, for any other form of government." (237)

"I know nothing about politics. . . . By being moderate and temperate in politics I suppose you mean being adroit, and doing that which is expedient and which will probably be successful. But the Church is founded on absolute truth, and teaches absolute truth, and there can be no compromise on such matters." (238)

And almost always Disraeli presents Nigel in a most favorable light.

Even though Endymion finally speaks out against Catholic influence in England and even though Nigel announces that the Catholic sphere will soon include England, both men debate at a level very different from the one I have been discussing. They are considering the political power plays of the Catholic and anti-Catholic forces, the kind of problem we have seen in *Lothair*. Although events bore out Nigel's position (the Catholic Church did legally establish its hierarchy in England in 1850), Disraeli was able to make a distinction between the ethos of the Church and its historically real presence. Generally, he was attracted by the former and repelled by the latter; he was obviously neither a quasi-Catholic nor an incipient convert. The fact remains, however, that, throughout his literary career, Disraeli found the traditional past—as he read it—a source of inspiration and solace; and the Catholic Church certainly occupied a position of great significance in that past. Throughout his life, Disraeli believed in the ultimate efficacy of tradition. In *Endymion*, Job Thornberry is a case in point.

The son of a farmer, Job was early in life caught up in the Society for the Diffusion of Knowledge, a radical political and economic organization. In his first conversations with Mr. Ferrars, Job argues in behalf of the most liberal, far-reaching change; and in this meeting and conversation Disraeli once again presents the conflict between change and the *status quo*:

Mr. Ferrars found Job not so manageable in controversy as his father. His views were peculiar, and his conclusions certain. He had more than a smattering too of political economy, a kind of knowledge which Mr. Ferrars viewed with suspicion; for though he had himself been looked upon as enlightened in this respect in the last years of Lord

Liverpool, when Lord Wallace and Mr. Huskisson were astonishing the world, he had relapsed, after the schism of the Tory party, into orthodoxy, and was satisfied that the tenets of the economists were mere theories, or could only be reduced into practice by revolution" (49).

Job goes on to become a significant radical leader and spokesman. Yet with success and financial security his world of values begins to undergo subtle changes until he finally becomes a gentleman-like land owner, his wife converts to the Catholic Church, and his son takes over the leadership of the High Church party in the Oxford Union. The critical fact here is that Job is not intellectually pleased with all of these changes, but he is emotionally satisfied by them: "His intelligence was as clear as ever, and his views on all subjects unchanged; but he was, like many other men, governed at home by his affections. He preferred the new arrangements if his wife and family were happy and contented . . ." (462).

Another case involves the Radical MP, Jorrocks, who is wined and exploited for his vote on a crucial issue. As in other similar cases in the novels, the aristocrats are sure they read Jorrocks' character perfectly: "He was a pretentious, underbred, half-educated man, fluent with all the commonplaces of middle-class ambition, which are humorously called democratic opinions, but at heart a sycophant of the aristocracy" (206). The fact is that in the cases of both Jorrocks and Thornberry—one knowledge-able, the other not—the pull of tradition runs as a strong counter-movement to their intellectual or announced commitments.

I have said that Disraeli responds to his lifelong commitment to tradition in a variety of terms in *Endymion*. His treatment of Catholicism and Job Thornberry are two, but the most obvious response in this novel is the author's re-creation of the historically real Eglinton Tournament as the Montfort Tournament. Can we not hear the Young England sentiment in Nigel Penruddock's assessment of the event? "I am thinking of what is beneath all this. . . . A great revivification. Chivalry is the child of the Church; it is the distinctive feature of Christian Europe. Had it not been for the revival of Church principles, this glorious pageant would never have occurred. But it is a pageant only to the uninitiated. There is not a ceremony, a form, a phrase, a costume, which is not symbolic of a great truth or a high purpose" (259). In this statement we find the younger Disraeli's belief in the value of ceremony and ritual and Sidonia's pronouncement on man's desire to obey in the narrator's remark on the close of the tournament's grand procession: "Every procession must end. It is a pity, for there is nothing so popular with mankind. The splendid part of the pageant had passed, but still the people gazed and looked as if they would have gazed for ever" (262).

In the midst of this novel's invocation of the manifold changes taking place in England, there is also another significant throwback to the Young England days as the *old* Tory party is indicted. What the relation may be between Disraeli's re-reading in 1880 of the earlier Tory party and his thoughtful explanation in 1870 of the purposes of the Young England novels must remain conjectural, but there is little doubt that the emotional and intellectual *milieu* of Young England remained with Disraeli. The fact that he dwells upon the questions of the 1840's in his last two novels is evidence enough.

And he deals with these problems in a most sympathetic manner in both the General Preface and in *Endymion*. From our first meeting with Zenobia, "the Queen of London, of fashion, and of the Tory party," we are given the opportunity to meet with the precise brand of Toryism scorned by Young England: fashionable, cliché-ridden, interested only in power and position. Having no principles, the Tory hierarchy is committed to its view of politics: to be the government rather than the opposition. Its conception of liberalism is bizarre: "It means the abolition of property and religion" (7). By a "renovated and restored" Tory party, Zenobia and her fellows mean that two powerful Whig members of the cabinet have been replaced by Tories. Their conception of preserving the public good involves the fight to keep gas lights from Grosvenor Square; since the country needs nothing of a substantial nature, lights for Grosvenor Square must be—from the Tory point of view—a significant issue.

Yet in this novel—unlike the Young England trilogy—the point of view is a Whig one. Perhaps Disraeli desired greater distance in *Endymion*, but by invoking a vantage point on the

Whig side he is able to more critically indict the Whigs also. On most issues they are little better than the old Tories and their key words, too, are conciliation and position. In the race for power and wealth, both parties abandon all previous commitments. Witness their response to the railroad boom: "Political connections, political consistency, political principle, all vanished before the fascination of premiums" (356).

Thus the last two complete novels return often to the thematic center of the Young England trilogy.[7] Of course, they do much more, for *Endymion,* in particular, is a rich novel for those interested in the nineteenth century. In it much of the age comes alive; and, as long as we realize the often special points of view held by the author, the experience of reading the novel is rewarding.[8]

III Falconet

To say that *Falconet* is Disraeli's unfinished novel is to overstate the case, for we have but thirty pages. Yet even in so short a fragment Disraeli was able to initiate at least two strands of subject matter which unquestionably would have been at the heart of the completed work: (1) the career of Joseph Toplady Falconet and (2) the ideological tension between Hartmann and Kusinara. Falconet himself was obviously modelled on Disraeli's greatest parliamentary enemy, William Ewart Gladstone; and from only thirty pages we can well imagine what Disraeli was going to do to Gladstone[9]—as the following descriptions and comments on Falconet indicate:

Joseph Toplady Falconet had been a child of singular precocity. His power of acquisition was remarkable, and, as he advanced in youth, his talents were evidently not merely those which ripen before their time. He was a grave boy, and scarcely ever known to smile; and this not so much from a want of sympathy for those among whom he was born and bred, for he seemed far from being incapable of domestic affection, but rather from a complete deficiency in the sense of humour, of which he seemed quite debarred. (474)

And what were the dreams of the youth himself? Had he any? Though of an eager and earnest temperament, his imagination was limited, and quite conscious of his powers, being, indeed, somewhat arrogant and peremptory, aspired only to devote them to accomplishing those objects which, from his cradle, he had been taught were the greatest, and the only ones, which could or should occupy the energies of man. (474-75)

Joseph Toplady Falconet was essentially a prig, and among prigs there is a free-masonry which never fails. All the prigs spoke of him as of the coming man. (490-91)

This element in the novel is clear-cut when compared with the other strand, the tension between Hartmann and Kusinara, which is so slightly developed and therefore so tenuous that it is clearly dangerous to attempt to make too much of it. Yet what we do have offers such fascinating possibilities that we can hardly ignore it. Kusinara, a half-Buddhist, half-Christian, has come to England to examine the decay of faith and to attempt a remedy, indeed "the great remedy which can alone cure the evils of the human race." The reader familiar with the entire Disraeli canon must be struck at this obvious analogue to Tancred. Only the geographical directions of the mission are different. Even though the spiritual crisis has not changed very much since the Young England days, Kusinara is hopeful; a universal remedy is possible. Hartmann, on the other hand, has a position less clearly articulated in these early pages of the novel.

We know that Hartmann and his nameless friend both believe that mankind is in a state of rapid decay. Their remedy involves what they call "the destruction of the species"—a meaningless phrase in terms of the fragment. But we nevertheless perceive that their view of motivating change through any political process and by conventional means is also strikingly like the position of Young England: "If anything is to be really done in this world, it must be done by visionaries; men who see the future, and make the future because they see it. What I really feared about him [apparently a leader in the movement] was that he had the weakness of believing in politics, of supposing that the pessimism of the universe could be changed or even modified by human arrangements" (496). Yet Hartmann distrusts religion (although he exploits it to reach his goals) and believes in some kind of destructive process after which a rebirth will be possible. These factors are clearly not in the Young England mold.

Thus the tension has been established early between Kusinara's optimistic and spiritual belief in remedying the ills of man and Hartmann's pessimistic and amoral sense of the predicament of man.

So the fragment ends. Where it would have finally gone is an unanswerable question because of the brevity of the manuscript. Yet I would conjecture that the Kusinara-Hartmann plot would have developed in a manner indicative of Disraeli's lately rekindled interest in Young England.

Epilogue

ONE of the major themes we have seen developed in the preceding chapters involves Disraeli's use of the past. In this area Disraeli was in the mainstream of a significant nineteenth-century mode of thought. One aspect of my discussion of his works—its analysis of his interest in tradition—should indicate a good deal about Disraeli's essentially little-known intelligence. Despite his public pronouncements and private correspondence, we know little more than the externals of the Prime Minister's life and thought. The particular fecundity of that mind seems always to have been artfully concealed from a too public view. To reveal one aspect of that mind, to lift away a portion of the concealing veil, has been one intention of this study. Through an awareness of Disraeli's historical and ideological bias, we come to a closer understanding of the writer and the man himself.

It is impossible to isolate any single cluster of sources as the primary agent in the growth of Disraeli's interest in the past. The years in which Disraeli matured were bristling with a variegated intellectualism; certainly one aspect of that intellectual tenor was geared to tradition. The Middle Ages, for instance, were of interest during the first four decades of the century; and this preoccupation resulted in historical studies and antiquarian societies. Furthermore, there is no question but that Isaac D'Israeli's love of history was passed on to his son. Things medieval and traditional were a major influence in much popular literature which Disraeli not only read but also discussed with his father's literary friends. In addition, Disraeli was greatly influenced by writers like Carlyle, Burke, and Coleridge. In summary, then, Disraeli's sense of the past is a result of a complex of factors: one aspect of the climate of opinion between

1800 and 1840, family and friends, and specific influential figures.
To find the Prime Minister's most extensive commitment to
the past, we must turn to the novels rather than to any other
product of Disraeli's intellect. His commitment is not thrust
upon us as overtly as Carlyle's in *Past and Present*, nor does his
life offer a key as does Morris's. Just as Disraeli concealed so
many of his other significant attitudes, so he offered his reading
of the past in oblique terms. We need only recall Disraeli's
response to the cleric who did not fathom the Asian mystery:
". . . as I have written three volumes to answer the question he
asks . . . recommend repeated, and frequent, study of the work
as the most efficient means for his purpose." We, too, have taken
the advice, for it is to precisely those three novels, the Young
England trilogy, that this study has been primarily directed.
From an analysis of *Coningsby, Sybil*, and *Tancred* I have indicated and illustrated their author's ideological orientation in his
view of history, society and politics, and religion.

Disraeli's view of history centers upon the organic, spiraling
nature of history. "For, put in its boldest terms, Disraeli's central
premiss about the human situation is . . . that human society as
a whole is a live thing. Its essential qualities are *continuity* and
vitality."[1] Like Burke, Carlyle, and Newman, Disraeli argues
forcefully in favor of the efficacy of tradition—of that which has
been tried, tested, and found successful. Abstractions in themselves are valueless unless they are abstracted from practice.
Essentially, Disraeli's reading of history underlies his views of
politics, society, and religion. Obviously, the areas of history and
religion are related in Disraeli's world view—as they must be—
since the organic, vital continuity to be seen in man's history is
in the final analysis welded to a religious framework. And it is
in the Young England novels that we have seen the most fully
developed products of Disraeli's traditional, even medieval sensi-
tivities. His biographers are correct when they suggest that,
"Revolutionary as he really was on one side of his complex
nature, there was another side. . . . Reverence for the past, a
semitic feeling for religion, an instinct for the positive, for order,
for tradition, for everything that Carlyle embodies in the phrase
'the everlasting yea'—all these things were strong within him,

and it was in their development and expression . . . that his mission really lay."[2]

We have seen that many of the motifs of the trilogy appeared in tentative form in several of the early novels and were still part of Disraeli's sensibilities in his last works. In this sense, the mission was with Disraeli for a half century. We can trace his commitments from their intimations in the early works, to their full conception and articulation in the Young England novels, to their presence—although often diluted or refined by the author's years of experience—in the last novels. Yet, as this study also indicates, Disraeli was more than a novelist with a mission. When we survey all of his novels, we cannot escape the realization that we are in the presence of a Disraeli-world in which characters and events from different novels come to share. One reason for this is the attention the author gives to history and politics, subjects which tend to bind most of the novels together. Thus the often brilliant imaginative recapitulation of an age to be found in Disraeli's novels must offer as striking a reason for examining those works as that to be discovered in the author's mission. Also, of course, there is the satire and humor which run throughout all the novels and which have managed to remain surprisingly fresh.

It is with the serious basis of the novels that I have dealt, and in such a discussion the tone of the novels could be misrepresented. To prevent misrepresentation, I must mention Disraeli's humor, albeit often wry humor. The Young England trilogy, for example, is fundamentally a serious attempt to articulate the program and credo of the movement. But, given Disraeli's wit and his sense of the ludicrous, as well as his occasional stumbles into melodrama, we must be on guard lest we read the novels *too* seriously and thus omit or overlook the humor in them. Conversely, we must not fall into the error of assuming that the novels of the trilogy are the mere exercises of a dexterous intellect or the frothy play of a man whose serious energies are engaged elsewhere. The most interesting and teasing problem in discussing Disraeli's humor resides in that middle area of ambiguity where we must ask whether the humor is present for its own sake (as it so often is) or whether the humor functions organically in terms of the novel's theme or plot. Thus when the reader comes to the end of *Tancred*, for instance, he must ask himself about the tone and "purpose" of the entrance of Tancred's relatives and friends on the very last page of the book. Does this invasion of English tourists point toward the long way the English aristocracy has to go before the symbolic meaning of the great Asian mystery can become fact, or is Disraeli—rarely willing to completely drop the witty touch—toying with or amusing his readers?

In their own right the Young England novels, as Professor Leavis has stated, deserve to be rediscovered. In the course of this discussion I have suggested the intellectual as well as the ideological breadth of those three works in addition to the numerous relationships between them and Disraeli's other fiction. And it is always to *Coningsby*, *Sybil*, and *Tancred* that the reader must return when attempting to assess Disraeli's importance as a novelist. Certainly in these novels we have Disraeli's primary significance as a novelist: in the trilogy he created the political novel.

Even though Disraeli is at times cynical or wry or pessimistic, Contarini Fleming's statement must also have been Disraeli's: "My interest in the happiness of my race is too keen to permit me for a moment to be blind to the storms that lour on the horizon of society. Perchance, also, the political regeneration of the country to which I am devoted may not be distant, and in that great work I am resolved to participate" (*Contarini Fleming*, 363). In his Young England novels we perceive the ideologically uncompromised Disraeli, and this Disraeli is often naïve and at times even foolish; but by no means should this fact call into question Disraeli's practical political acumen. Although his politics and his literary creations are both parts of the essential Disraeli, his novels and their "solutions" to problems generally move on an abstract and certainly imaginative plane. Yet, as late as 1870, Disraeli could still say of the Young England novels: "They recognised imagination in the government of nations as a quality not less important than reason."[3]

Notes and References

Preface
1. F. R. Leavis, *The Great Tradition* (New York, 1954), p. 10.

Chapter 1
1. Quoted in William F. Monypenny and George E. Buckle, *The Life of Benjamin Disraeli, Earl of Beaconsfield* (London, 1929), I, 27. Hereafter referred to as Monypenny and Buckle.
2. For a fuller treatment of the subjects which I merely sketch here, see, for example, Jerome Hamilton Buckley's *The Victorian Temper* (Cambridge, 1951) and Walter E. Houghton's *The Victorian Frame of Mind* (New Haven, 1957).
3. Monypenny and Buckle, I, 14.
4. J. A. Froude, *Lord Beaconsfield* (London, 1891), p. 12.
5. Monypenny and Buckle, I, 16.
6. George K. Anderson, "Isaac Disraeli's *Amenities of Literature:* A Centennial Review," *Philological Quarterly,* XXII (April, 1943), 103.
7. *Ibid.,* p. 100.
8. See note 5 under Chapter 4, "Meaning in History."
9. B. R. Jerman, *The Young Disraeli* (Princeton, 1960), pp. 41-2.
10. *Ibid.,* p. 42.
11. "Benjamin D'Israeli the elder remained to the end of his life a member of the Sephardi congregation of Bevis Marks, and though as we are told [Picciotto's *Sketches of Anglo-Jewish History,* p. 295], he was somewhat lax in his observances and took no great interest in the affairs of the synagogue, he contributed liberally to its support and gave increased donations as the growth of his fortune gave warrant. On one occasion he even served in the minor office of Inspector of the Charity School . . ." Monypenny and Buckle, I, 11.
12. Isaac D'Israeli, quoted in Cecil Roth, *Benjamin Disraeli* (New York, 1952), pp. 18-9.
13. D. L. Murray, *Disraeli* (London, 1927), p. 22.
14. *Ibid.*
15. Roth, pp. 22-3.

16. Froude, p. 169.

17. See particularly Monypenny and Buckle, Book I; Hesketh Pearson, *Dizzy*; and B. R. Jerman, *The Young Disraeli*, the first full-length study of Disraeli's early years.

18. *Athenaeum* (May 12, 1832), p. 307.

19. Kathleen Tillotson, *Novels of the Eighteen Forties* (Oxford, 1954), p. 124.

20. *Ibid.*

21. Benjamin Disraeli, *Coningsby*, p. xviii. All references to the novels of Disraeli are to the Bradenham Edition, edited by Philip Guedalla, 12 volumes (London, 1926-27).

22. Monypenny and Buckle, I, 560.

23. In these decades there was an increasing popular interest in the past. The interest in the Gothic and in the Middle Ages was, of course, not limited to historians and antiquarian societies. (See, for example, Robert Preyer, *Bentham, Coleridge, and the Science of History*; Richard Altick, *The English Common Reader*; R. A. E. Brooks, "The Development of the Historical Mind" in *The Reinterpretation of Victorian Literature*, edited by Joseph E. Baker; Kenneth Clark, *The Gothic Revival*; R. G. Collingwood, *The Idea of History*; T. P. Peardon, *The Transition in English Historical Writing*; Harrison R. Steeves, *Learned Societies and English Literary Scholarship*; G. P. Gooch, *History and Historians in the Nineteenth Century*.)

In imaginative literature, the eighteenth century showed a re-awakened interest in the past. The Gothic novel, Strawberry Hill, Gray, Warton, Hurd's *Letters on Chivalry and Romance* (1762), Percy's *Reliques of Ancient English Poetry* (1765), the fascinating Chatterton—all of these represent the pre-Romantic movement of the eighteenth century. The Romantics, without question, concerned themselves with the past and with the Middle Ages. Kenneth Clark sees the interest in Gothic architecture as a symptom of the Romantic movement; and he adds that "any definition [of the Romantic movement] must suggest that the Middle Ages took the place of classical times as an ideal in art and letters" (*The Gothic Revival*, p. 87).

Sir Walter Scott's novels spread the medieval sentiment and struck the imagination of millions of Englishmen. Scott was the most successful of the historical novelists of the age; and his *Ivanhoe* was published in 1819, followed by *The Monastery* in 1820 and *Woodstock* in 1826. Yet even before the publication of these novels, Gothic archeology had become immensely popular. "It is hard to believe that so dry a subject could become popular in any sense in which *Ivanhoe* was popular. But we know from our own day how the most abstruse subjects can suddenly strike the public imagination; and from 1800 to 1820 a flood of pamphlets shows that Gothic archeology was a craze . . ." (*The Gothic Revival*, p. 95).

The literacy rate in England was steadily increasing during the nineteenth century, and the interest in the past spread to the middle classes. The effects of more highly mechanized methods of printing and lower priced printed products have been noted by many. Robert Chambers wrote in 1836: "Several London booksellers . . . commenced the publication [in 1823] of cheap weekly sheets, either containing portions of some standard books; or a series of miscellaneous literary articles, chiefly extracted from other works" (*History of the English Language and Literature*, pp. 269-70). An Irish literary historian, J. Hamilton Fyfe, wrote in 1878: "The influence of the great change—the substitution of the steam *printing-press* for the hand-worked *printing-press*—has been felt in every corner of the land, where a cheap book or penny newspaper has found its way" (W. F. Collier, *A History of English Literature*, p. 440).

Richard Altick wrote in 1957: "Only as the market expanded were mass-production techniques found practicable; but once they were introduced, they brought down costs, and the cheapening of books. . . . Taking full advantage of steam printing and stereotypes, he [William Clowes] was the great pioneer of mass-produced books and periodicals. In the 1830's and 1840's steam replaced hand operations throughout the book-printing trade" (*The English Common Reader*, p. 277). As the reading public quickly increased, lending libraries opened and soon were doing booming business. Indeed, scanning the "Best Sellers" list in Altick's *The English Common Reader* (pp. 381-90) gives the reader a glimpse of the tremendous numbers of books bought, which when coupled to the vast numbers rented indicates graphically the extent of the reading public.

There were other areas of scholarship and art which aided in heightening the interest in the past of England. Histories of literature started to become popular items in the book market. Robert Chambers' *Cyclopedia of English Literature* (1833-34) sold 130,000 copies in a few years, a considerable figure even today for a history of literature. R. A. E. Brooks points out that the museums and galleries played a significant role in spreading knowledge about the past throughout the middle classes: "In these museums and galleries were paintings which certainly reflect both the growing awareness of the past and the growing nationalism" ("The Development of the Historical Mind," p. 144). Brooks adds that the artistry of the paintings is not a real consideration in this context, but rather the significant consideration is the success which the art met with in bringing middle-class Englishmen to visualize the past.

The reawakening to history is one aspect of the England into which Benjamin Disraeli was born and by which he was so greatly influenced. He read widely and discussed freely. His father, one sometimes thinks, read everything. Isaac's library was Benjamin's playground; Isaac's literary friends were Benjamin's first intellectual playmates. That England was in such a state of historical inquiry was obviously fortunate, for Disraeli's sensibilities were satisfied by such a congenial enterprise.

24. John Holloway, *The Victorian Sage* (London, 1953), p. 87.

25. Too many Disraeli commentators have stressed a close biographical reading of the novels. That glimpses of Disraeli can be seen in his novels is true, but there is little more to be done in this area. Monypenny and Buckle and other writers (Hesketh Pearson, Cecil Roth, B. R. Jerman, and Georg Brandes, for example) have carried this pursuit a good distance. Where they have been wrong, they should be corrected; but further biographical readings of Disraeli's novels must be approached with one simple question: does the thesis of the study validate the biographical reading? I am afraid that there are not many such theses remaining.

26. Walter Allen, *The English Novel* (New York, 1955), p. 178.

27. V. S. Pritchett, *The Living Novel* (New York, 1947), pp. 77-8.

28. André Maurois, *Disraeli* (New York, 1936), p. 257.

29. Bismarck on Disraeli: "Der Alte Jude, das ist der Mann." The following line from Homer was inscribed under a portrait of Disraeli hanging at the Conservatives Club in London: "He alone is wise, the rest are fleeting shades."

Chapter 2

1. For full summaries of the novels see Monypenny and Buckle, and Muriel Masefield's *Peacocks and Primroses* (London, 1953).

2. Though perhaps no narrative intrusion is as deplorable as pp. 113-14 in *Coningsby* where Disraeli literally asks for funds for Eton's library.

3. Notably *Popanilla* (1828) which discusses politics but not seriously.

4. The Duke's visit to the cottagers includes no social comment by the author. There is, however, at least an *awareness* of cottagers and their way of life. Disraeli introduces the cottagers here as Jane Austen does in *Emma*. Not until the Young England novels does Disraeli come to sound like Dickens on such subjects.

5. We might argue that these are intrusions more typical of some nineteenth-century novelists rather than of a youthful novelist. How-

ever, few mature Victorian novelists are guilty of such narrative commentary which is witty without being tasteful or functional. Compare only the early and the mature Disraeli to see the differences in his handling of narrative technique.

6. See Kathleen Tillotson's *Novels of the Eighteen Forties* for the changes taking place in the novel.

7. "Here let me pass my life in the study and the creation of the beautiful. Such is my desire; but whether it will be my career is, I feel, doubtful. My interest in the happiness of my race is too keen to permit me for a moment to be blind to the storms that lour on the horizon of society. Perchance also the political regeneration of the country to which I am devoted may not be distant, and in that great work I am resolved to participate. Bitter jest, that the most civilised portion of the globe should be considered incapable of self-government!

"When I examine the state of European society with the unimpassioned spirit which the philosopher can alone command, I perceive that it is in a state of transition from feudal to federal principles. This I conceive to be the sole and secret cause of all the convulsions that have occurred or are to occur.

"Circumstances are beyond the control of man; but his conduct is in his own power. The great event is as sure as that I am now penning this prophecy of its occurrence. With us it rests whether it shall be welcomed by wisdom or by ignorance, whether its beneficent results shall be accelerated by enlightened minds, or retarded by our dark passions.

"What is the arch of the conqueror, what the laurel of the poet! I think of the infinity of space, I feel my nothingness. Yet if I am to be remembered, let me be remembered as one who, in a sad night of gloomy ignorance and savage bigotry was prescient of the flaming morning-break of bright philosophy, as one who deeply sympathised with his fellow-men, and felt a proud and profound conviction of their perfectibility; as one who devoted himself to the amelioration of his kind, by the destruction of error and the propagation of truth." (*Contarini Fleming*, pp. 363-64).

8. Philip Guedalla, "A Note on 'Alroy,'" *Alroy* (Bradenham Edition, London, 1927), p. vi.

9. This reading of *Alroy* does no harm to the biographical factors inherent in the novel. Certainly one can imagine Disraeli, an alien, lamenting the state of his frustrated ambitions in Alroy's terms: "And even now a vivid flash darts through the darkness of my mind. Methinks, methinks: ah! worst of woes to dream of glory in despair. No, no; I live and die a most ignoble thing; beauty and love, and fame

and mighty deeds, the smile of women and the gaze of men, and the ennobling consciousness of worth, and all the fiery course of the creative passions, these are not for me, and I, Alroy, the descendant of sacred kings, and with a soul that pants for empire, I stand here extending my vain arm for my lost sceptre, a most dishonoured slave!" (p. 9).

10. View the episodes on the following pages of the novel for examples: 43, 55, 88, 90, 92, 93, 96, 97.

11. The sharp differences between Jabaster and Honain are here made clear in terms of plot. Honain views the events of the previous evening's interview between Alroy and Jabaster in perfectly rational terms—and at this moment Alroy wants nothing but such an explanation. However, given the events of the past, the novel clearly suggests that Alroy is foolish to discard Jabaster's reading of events and of the entire mystical environment in which they both operated so successfully.

12. We might even argue here that Alroy is saved from a torturous death by his return to commitment.

13. Quoted by Philip Guedalla in "A Note on 'Venetia,'" *Venetia* (Bradenham Edition, London, 1927), p. vii.

14. In one sense, of course, this view of the artist as a man of letters vitally concerned with the great non-literary problems of his times is a generally accepted notion in nineteenth-century England. In another sense, however, the same view in the works of a practicing politician must take on significant biographical interest.

15. Just before Cadurcis meets Herbert, the narrator says: "Society had outraged him [Cadurcis], and now he resolved to outrage society" (343).

Chapter 3

1. For a sensible re-assessment of this whole matter of the "middle class," see G. Kitson Clark, *The Making of Victorian England* (Cambridge, 1962), especially pp. 5-7, 118-23.

2. See, for example, Clyde J. Lewis, "Theory and Expediency in the Politics of Disraeli," *Victorian Studies,* IV (March, 1961), 237-58.

3. Benjamin Disraeli, "General Preface by the Author to the Collected Edition of his Novels published in 1870, and known as the Hughenden Edition," *Novels and Tales* (Bradenham Edition, London, 1926), I, x.

4. *Ibid.,* p. xiii.

5. *Ibid.,* p. xii.

6. Charles F. Harrold and William D. Templeman, *English Prose of the Victorian Era* (New York, 1954), p. xlix.

7. Kathleen Tillotson, *Novels of the Eighteen Forties* (Oxford, 1954), pp. 122-23.

8. See note 16 under Chapter Five, "Society and Religion."

9. Even though the particular interpretation of the hero varied with the interpreter (Coleridge, Burke, Scott, Carlyle, Disraeli, etc.), the essential heroic characteristics remain constant.

10. See R. W. and A. J. Carlyle, *A History of Mediaeval Political Theory in the West* (Edinburgh, 1916), III, 92-3, 182-83.

11. Frederick B. Artz, *The Mind of the Middle Ages* (New York, 1954), p. 455.

12. Disraeli, "General Preface," p. xi.

13. Monypenny and Buckle, I, 699.

14. R. B. McDowell, *British Conservatism, 1832-1914* (London, 1959), p. 17.

15. Asa Briggs, *The Age of Improvement, 1783-1867* (New York, 1960), p. 332.

16. Gregory Zilboorg, *Mind, Medicine, and Man* (New York, 1943), p. 218.

17. Karl Löwith indicates the kind of "movement" I am discussing when he speaks of Comte's view of the same problem: "To counterbalance the anarchical trend of mere progression toward individual rights (instead of common duties), abstract liberty (instead of voluntary subordination), and equality (instead of hierarchy) and to terminate the revolutionary period of the last centuries, the stabilizing force of order has to be reorganized; for only a system which unites order with progress can direct the revolutionary state, which has been characteristic of Europe's history since the dissolution of the order of the Middle Ages, towards its final and positive term" (*Meaning in History*, p. 67).

18. Herbert J. Muller, *The Uses of the Past* (New York, 1952), pp. 238-39. Here again, of course, there is an historical tension regarding the nature of the Middle Ages. Muller's view underscores Disraeli's, but there are opposing views held by commentators such as Johan Huizinga who sees the Middle Ages as more pluralistic and diverse than Disraeli *imagined* the period to be.

19. One of the obvious problems in approaching Disraeli is the reader's realization that the novelist's world view transcends his abilities to incorporate it within a significant and major artistic vehicle.

Chapter 4

1. Harold J. Laski, *Studies in the Problem of Sovereignty* (New Haven, 1917), p. 64.

2. Benjamin Disraeli, "Vindication of the English Constitution," *Whigs and Whiggism,* ed. William Hutcheon (New York, 1924), p. 120.

3. That the Saint-Simonians had a real influence on English thought can be shown clearly by indicating the relationship between them and Carlyle. Hill Shine points out several of the many scholars who have noted this influence (*Carlyle and the Saint Simonians*). As early as 1903, the correspondence between Carlyle and the Saint-Simonians was published (Eugene d'Eichthal, "Carlyle et la Saint-Simonisme"). Bougle and Halévy felt that Carlyle was a conscious disciple of Saint-Simon (*Doctrine de Saint-Simon*). D. A. Wilson considered Saint-Simon's *Nouveau Christianisme* as "a stimulant to the expansion of *Sartor*" (*Carlyle to the "French Revolution,"* p. 190). Emery Neff saw *Sartor Resartus* as "almost entirely a synthesis of the ideas of the German philosophers and the Saint-Simonians" (*Carlyle and Mill,* p. 217). Neff also felt that Saint-Simon's thought was a "clarifier of many ideas which had been struggling for expression in his [Carlyle's] own mind" (*Ibid.,* p. 215). Shine, himself, feels that the Saint-Simonian views influenced to a great extent Carlyle's concept of history. See also note 5 following.

4. Disraeli and the Coleridgean view is developed in greater detail in my text.

5. There is no precise information as to the nature of Disraeli's reading. However, there are several indications of the direction it took. We know that his father's immense personal library was at Benjamin's disposal. Of all his possessions, Isaac D'Israeli valued his books most. "He often said to his son, 'the Octavos are my Infantry, my Cavalry are the Quartos, and the Folios are my Artillery.' There were 25,000 volumes in all, of which Disraeli transferred the best to Hughenden [after the death of Isaac], but the larger part were sold" (Monypenny and Buckle, I, 961).

A more particular statement of Disraeli's major interests in reading is found in the following note about his beloved Hughenden existence whenever he could get away from the pressures of the city: "I have a passion for books and trees. I like to look at them. When I come down to Hughenden I pass the first week in sauntering about my park and examining all the trees, and then I saunter in the library and survey the books. *My collection is limited to Theology, the Classics, and History.* Anything miscellaneous in it is the remains of the Bradenham Collection, but the great bulk of the Belles-Lettres I parted with after my father's death [January 19, 1848]" (Monypenny and Buckle, I, 973-74, italics mine). Late in life in his retirement (about 1879), Disraeli's favorite reading was "classics of either Latin, Italian Renais-

Notes and References

sance, or English eighteenth-century Literature" (Monypenny and Buckle, II, 1509).

Carlyle's influence on Disraeli is not only obvious to anyone who has read both writers, but has been commented on by several readers. J. A. Froude, who knew both men, says that Disraeli "had studied Carlyle, and in some of his writings had imitated him. Carlyle did not thank him for this. Carlyle detested Jews, and looked on Disraeli as an adventurer fishing for fortune in Parliamentary waters. . . . Nevertheless, Disraeli had taken his teaching to heart, and in his own way meant to act upon it. He regarded the aristocracy, like Carlyle also . . . as the least corrupted part of the community; and to them, in alliance with the people, he looked for a return of the English nation to the lines of true progress" (*Lord Beaconsfield*, p. 84). "The opinions of Benjamin Disraeli, if we take *Sybil* for their exponent, were the opinions of the author of *Past and Present*" (*Ibid.*, p. 92). Furthermore, we know that through Disraeli, Carlyle was offered the Grand Cross of the Bath in recognition of his work. This award had never before been conferred on any English author. Carlyle refused, but Disraeli's estimate of Carlyle is clearly seen by virtue of the offer.

6. See Hill Shine, *Carlyle and the Saint Simonians* (Baltimore, 1941), pp. 156-75, 178-79.

7. Samuel Taylor Coleridge, *The Table Talk and Omniana of Samuel Taylor Coleridge* (London, 1917), p. 106.

8. Quoted in Monypenny and Buckle, I, 185.

9. *Ibid.*, I, 200.

10. Robert Preyer, *Bentham, Coleridge, and the Science of History* (Bochum-Langendreer, Western Germany, 1958), p. 89. Throughout this Chapter, I am indebted to Preyer's excellent study.

11. *Ibid.*, p. 45.

12. *Ibid.*, p. 46.

13. Arnold and Hare grew pessimistic about the future. Although they agreed with Coleridge that the spirit of history was moral and that the state was an organic entity historically, they were greatly shaken by the facts of contemporary life. License rather than restraint seemed to rule their fellow men. The economic system, the social structure, and the religious establishment were all falling away from the spirit of morality. Arnold and Hare lamented the lack of Christian ideals in operation in the lives of men. Across the channel, the German counterparts of the Coleridgeans had moved further than pessimism and had fallen into utter despair. Listen to B. G. Niebuhr in 1830: "We have fallen into the state of Rome after the times of the Gracchi, with all its horrors, and he who cannot see this is blind. . . . That it was possible for reasonable men to do this, I had comprehended long

ago; now, it is perfectly vividly clear to me . . ." (*The Life and Letters of Barthold Georg Niebuhr*, p. 528). Listen to Ernst Troeltsch in 1848:

> The old pantheistic deification of the State became a blind worship of success and power; the Romantic Revolt sinks into a complacent contentment with things as they are. . . . Henceforth the political thought of Germany is marked by a curious dualism. . . . Look at one of its sides, and you will see an abundance of remnants of Romanticism and lofty idealism: Look to the other, and you will see a realism which goes to the verge of cynicism and of utter indifference to all ideals and all morality . . . above all, an inclination to make an astonishing combination of the two elements—in a word, to brutalize romance, and to romanticize cynicism. ("The Idea of Natural Law and Humanity in World Politics," p. 214)

14. Alfred Cobban, *Edmund Burke and the Revolt Against the Eighteenth Century* (London, 1929), p. 179.

15. Indeed, the epigraph (from *Troilus and Cressida*) to *The Constitution of the Church and State in Accordance with the Idea of Each* (1829) represents the core of Coleridge's historical view: "There is a mystery in the soul of state,/ Which hath an operation more divine/ Than our mere chroniclers dare meddle with." Coleridge's most significant contribution to the new historiography was that the nation is responsible for the moral cultivation and advancement of the people. What Coleridge has done, then, is to superimpose a spiritual dimension to the plan which shapes history. The nation emerges as a spiritual and moral organism. And it is the duty of the third estate, the Clergy, "to secure and improve the civilization, without which the nation could be neither permanent nor progressive" (*On the Constitution of the Church and State, Lay Sermons*, pp. 46-47).

16. Karl Löwith, *Meaning in History* (Chicago, 1949), p. 67.

17. *Ibid.*, p. 84.

18. Jacques Maritain, *On the Philosophy of History* (New York, 1957), pp. 120-23.

19. Carl Becker, "Progress," *The Encyclopedia of the Social Sciences* (New York, 1934), XII, 498.

20. *Ibid.*, p. 495.

21. *Ibid.*, p. 496.

22. Raymond Williams, *Culture and Society 1780-1950* (New York, 1958), p. 9.

23. *Ibid.*, p. 10.

24. R. G. Collingwood, *The Idea of History* (Oxford, 1946), p. 56.

Chapter 5

1. Lewis Mumford, *The Condition of Man* (New York, 1944), p. 150.
2. Kenneth Clark, *The Gothic Revival* (London, 1950), p. 197.
3. Mumford, p. 150.
4. *Ibid.*, p. 151.
5. Alfred North Whitehead, *The Dialogues of Alfred North Whitehead*, recorded by Lucien Price (Boston, 1954), p. 262.
6. Thirty years after the publication of *Tancred*, Disraeli announced the view noted to Jowett. (Monypenny and Buckle, I, 864.)
7. Leslie Stephen, *Hours in a Library* (London, 1899), II, 129.
8. Morris E. Speare, *The Political Novel* (New York, 1924), p. 88.
9. Among the better treatments of aspects of *Tancred* and/or Disraeli's thought reflected in that novel are the following (although none offers a full reading of the novel): Georg Brandes, *Lord Beaconsfield* (New York, 1880); Morris E. Speare, *The Political Novel* (New York, 1924); Frank Swinnerton, "Disraeli as Novelist," *Yale Review,* XVII (Jan., 1928), 283-300; Eric Forbes-Boyd, "Disraeli the Novelist," *Essays and Studies*, 1950, ed. G. R. Hamilton (London, 1950); John Holloway, *The Victorian Sage* (New York, 1953); Raymond Williams, *Culture and Society 1780-1950* (New York, 1958); and, of course, Monypenny and Buckle.
10. Monypenny and Buckle, I, 850.
11. Speare, pp. 94-5. Speare also suggests *One Hundred Cartoons for Mr. Punch* (London, 1878), which are mainly of Disraeli and many uncomplimentary within a religious framework.
12. *Ibid.*, p. 96.
13. Disraeli wrote that the general purpose of *Tancred* was to show "the duties of the Church as a main remedial agency in our present state" ("General Preface," p. xiii).
14. Monypenny and Buckle, I, 857.
15. Speare, p. 83.
16. Even though we learn at the end of the novel that Sybil herself is an aristocrat, the symbolic value of the marriage remains clear. The point is that, until the end of the book, Egremont is never aware of Sybil except as a member of the "people." Thus what he says and sometimes orates to her throughout the novel not only illustrates the responsibilities of the aristocracy as Young England defined them, but his desire to marry her is precisely the desire of the new Toryism symbolically presented, the desire to unite the two nations.
17. J. A. Froude has reported that Disraeli thought of Christianity

as completed Judaism: ". . . those who profess to be Jews only he [Disraeli] considers unfortunate in believing only the first part of their religion . . ." J. A. Froude, *Lord Beaconsfield* (London, 1891), p. 169.

18. Again the Baroni family affords a microcosmic view. Father Baroni says to Sidonia, "I rule and regulate my house like a ship." John Holloway adds that "the children honour their parents, the family lives by an ordered system of invariable rules, and all pursue those arts which are their traditional mode of livelihood." (*The Victorian Sage*, p. 93.)

19. Clyde J. Lewis comments on Disraeli's view of Christianity in the following manner:

> One may conclude . . . that the only progress Disraeli saw in history was quantitative. Man, in his view, had not been able to improve upon the eternal principles; but as time passed, more men had come to understand and apply God's laws. Individual states had risen and had fallen in the past, as different peoples had succeeded or failed in making the application. Yet from the beginning of the Christian era, a slowly but steadily growing awareness of God had shown itself among all peoples, as was demonstrated by the spreading permanence of Christianity. In the whole process, Disraeli saw the hand of God working through the Divine instrumentality of race. ("Disraeli's Conception of Divine Order," p. 155.)

Lewis' last sentence, I would suggest, is another way of stating Disraeli's conception of a spiraling pattern in the historical process.

Chapter 6

1. Monypenny and Buckle, II, 1439-40.
2. *Ibid.*, II, 489.
3. This remark does operate at a sociological level in that many people obviously shared the view, but it remains insignificant in terms of the novel.
4. I am reminded here of Marmion Herbert's lines in *Venetia*: ". . . why should we be surprised that the nature of man should change? Does not everything change? Is not change the law of nature? My skin changes every year, my hair never belongs to me a month, the nail on my hand is only a passing possession. I doubt whether a man at fifty is the same material being that he is at five-and-twenty" (pp. 436-37).
5. Similarly, when confronted with an elaborately conceived metaphor the reader can become caught up in the figure and move farther

and farther away from that which the figure represents. So with sustained satire. Indeed, how many college freshmen have been moved to the point of accepting Swift's modest proposal simply because of the sustained quality of its satire?

6. Philip Guedalla, "A Note on 'Endymion' and 'Falconet,'" *Endymion* (Bradenham Edition, London, 1927), p. ix.

7. Nor has Disraeli in 1880 forgotten the subject of race. His invocation of the special characteristics of the Hebrew race (p. 246) is as intense as was Eva's in *Tancred*.

8. Two examples of Disraeli's special point of view which I have not mentioned previously are Lord Roehampton and St. Barbe. Roehampton, modelled on Palmerston, emerges as an engaging portrait of a man Disraeli obviously admired greatly. St. Barbe, modelled on Thackeray, shows that the old politician had not mellowed to the benignity of old age.

9. Often in letters Disraeli referred to Gladstone as the A.V., for arch-villain.

Epilogue

1. John Holloway, *The Victorian Sage* (London, 1953), p. 88.
2. Monypenny and Buckle, I, 249.
3. "General Preface," p. xv.

Selected Bibliography

WORKS BY DISRAELI

Fiction

Vivian Grey. Vols. I and II, London: Colburn, 1826; Vols. III and IV, London: Colburn, 1827.

The Voyage of Captain Popanilla. London: Colburn, 1828.

The Young Duke. 3 vols., London: Colburn and Bentley, 1831.

Contarini Fleming: A Psychological Romance. 4 vols., London: Murray, 1832.

The Wondrous Tale of Alroy and The Rise of Iskander. 3 vols., London: Saunders and Otley, 1833.

Henrietta Temple: A Love Story. 3 vols., London: Colburn, 1837.

Venetia. 3 vols., London: Colburn, 1837.

Coningsby: Or The New Generation. 3 vols., London: Colburn, 1844.

Sybil: Or The Two Nations. 3 vols., London: Colburn, 1845.

Tancred: Or The New Crusade. 3 vols., London: Colburn, 1847.

Lothair. 3 vols., London: Longmans, 1870.

Endymion. 3 vols., London: Longmans, 1880.

Tales and Sketches, with a Prefatory Memoir by J. Logie Robertson. London: Paterson, 1891.

Selected Poetry

The Revolutionary Epick. 2 vols., London: Moxon, 1834.

The Tragedy of Count Alarcos. London: Colburn, 1839.

The Dunciad of To-Day; A Satire (Here Attributed to Disraeli) and, The Modern Aesop, with an introduction by Michael Sadleir. London: Ingpen and Grant, 1928. (It is Sadleir's assumption that this is Disraeli's work.)

Selected Political Writings and Speeches

Vindication Of The English Constitution In A Letter To A Noble And Learned Lord. London: Saunders and Otley, 1835.

Lord George Bentinck: A Political Biography. London: Colburn, 1852.

Bibliography

Speeches on the Conservative Policy of the Last Thirty Years, ed. J. F. Bulley. London: Hotten, 1870.

Selected Speeches, with notes by T. E. Kebbel. 2 vols., London: Longmans, 1882.

Whigs and Whiggism: Political Writings, ed. William Hutcheon. London: Murray, 1913. Includes: *What is He?* 1833; *The Crisis Examined*, 1834; *Vindication of the English Constitution*, 1835; *Letters of Runnymede*, 1836; *The Spirit of Whiggism*, 1836.

The Radical Tory: Disraeli's Political Development Illustrated from his Original Writings and Speeches, ed. H. W. J. Edwards. London: Cape, 1937.

Selected Letters

Lord Beaconsfield's Letters, 1830-1852. London: Murray, 1887. Includes: *Home Letters, 1830-31*, 1885, and *Disraeli's Correspondence With His Sister*, 1886. Edited by A. Birrell, London: Cassell, 1928.

Letters of Disraeli to Lady Bradford and Lady Chesterfield, ed. Marquis of Zetland. 2 vols., London: Benn, 1929.

Letters to Frances Anne, Marchioness of Londonderry, 1837-1861, ed. Marchioness of Londonderry. London: Macmillan, 1938.

SECONDARY SOURCES

Aronstein, Philipp. "Benjamin Disraelis Leben und dichterische Werke," *Anglia*, XVII (1895), 261-395. One of the few book-length studies of the novels. Aronstein is best when treating the relationship between Disraeli and Judaism. He also points toward the influence of Carlyle on Disraeli.

Blake, Robert. *Disraeli*. New York: St. Martin's, 1967. This brilliant study must be considered *the* biography of Disraeli. Blake "demythologizes" his subject, and in the process a supremely interesting and meaningful figure emerges. There seems little likelihood that a superior life of Disraeli will be produced.

Bloomfield, Paul. *Disraeli*. Writers and Their Work: No. 138. London: Longmans, 1961. Considering the fact that Bloomfield attempts to survey Disraeli's writing in only thirty pages, he deserves at least a nod for courage. However, the essay is recent and readable.

Brandes, Georg. *Lord Beaconsfield*. New York: Scribner's, 1880. This early treatment of Disraeli is interesting for two reasons. Brandes develops his thesis that the author's political career is closely related to the ideas inherent in the novels, and he often mentions

Disraeli's concern for the Middle Ages. This is one of the important early books on Disraeli.

Cazamian, Louis. *Le Roman social en Angleterre (1830-1850): Dickens, Disraeli, Mrs. Gaskell, Kingsley.* 2 vols., Paris: Société nouvelle de libraire et d'édition, 1904. As always, Cazamian is richly rewarding. In this study he treats the social ideas developed by Disraeli in his novels.

Frietzsche, Arthur H. *Disraeli's Religion: The Treatment of Religion in Disraeli's Novels.* Logan: Utah State University Press, 1961. Survey of the novels in which Frietzsche argues that Disraeli was continually seeking a religious position rather than operating from any firm religious conviction. See Clyde Lewis for a more convincing handling of the same general subject.

———. *The Monstrous Clever Young Man: The Novelist Disraeli and His Heroes.* Logan: Utah State University Press, 1959. Frietzsche's thesis rests on his assumption that Vivian Grey is "the archetype of a *genre*, the Disraeli-hero." His original proposition that Disraeli's heroes undergo a similar developmental pattern is generally a valid hypothesis, but Frietzsche fails to discuss the very significant refinements which are often present in that pattern. Nevertheless, this is an interesting study.

Froude, J. A. *Lord Beaconsfield.* London: Dent, 1891. An interesting and significant book since Froude knew both Disraeli and Carlyle, and he points to the considerable influence Carlyle exerted on Disraeli the novelist.

Graubard, Stephen. *Burke, Disraeli, Churchill: The Politics of Perseverance.* Cambridge: Harvard University Press, 1961. Although this study is essentially a political one, Graubard underscores Disraeli's reliance on the individual.

Harrison, Frederic. *Studies in Early Victorian Literature.* London: E. Arnold, 1895. Harrison's essay on Disraeli is generally pedestrian, but he does develop a cogent argument in behalf of Disraeli's merit as a novelist, a merit which has been overshadowed by his political stature.

Holloway, John. *The Victorian Sage.* New York: Macmillan, 1953. Holloway's chapter on Disraeli is easily one of the few important studies of Disraeli. His argument in behalf of Disraeli as sage is effective as it is often exciting. See my text for a few of Holloway's major points.

James, Stanley B. "The Tragedy of Disraeli," *Catholic World*, CLII (1941), 414-19. Although James is principally interested in trying to account for Disraeli's ultimate failure, he offers some interesting comments on Disraeli and Catholicism.

Bibliography

Jerman, B. R. *The Young Disraeli*. Princeton: Princeton University Press, 1960. An important study of Disraeli's early life (to 1837) in which Jerman sheds light on the role of the Austens and of Disraeli's financial difficulties. Much biographical confusion is cleared up by this book.

Lewis, Clyde J. "Disraeli's Conception of Divine Order." *Jewish Social Studies*, XXIV (July, 1962), 144-61. For the thesis of this excellent essay, see my note 19 to Chapter 5.

——. "Theory and Expediency in the Policy of Disraeli," *Victorian Studies*, IV (March, 1961), 237-58. A good article which—when read in conjunction with the novels—should highlight one aspect of the tension between the imaginative and real facts, between Disraeli's novels and his life.

MacKnight, Thomas. *The Right Honourable Benjamin Disraeli, M. P., A Literary and Political Biography*. London: Bentley, 1854. A good example of the hostility Disraeli generated in his own time: MacKnight views Disraeli as a charlatan and an atheist whose very political presence endangers the nation's future.

Masefield, Muriel. *Peacocks and Primroses: A Survey of Disraeli's Novels*. London: G. Bles, 1953. A survey of the novels that is very good indeed for plot summaries, but for those only.

Maurois, André. *Disraeli*. New York: Appleton-Century-Crofts, 1936. Romantic rendering of Disraeli's life that is often charming, but just as often unconvincing.

Monypenny, William F. and George E. Buckle. *The Life of Benjamin Disraeli, Earl of Beaconsfield*. 2 vols., London: Macmillan, 1929. Until the arrival of Robert Blake's *Disraeli*, this was the standard biography. Not only will the reader learn a good deal about the man and the writer in these volumes, but he will also gain a broad introduction to the age.

Murray, D. L. *Disraeli*. London: Benn, 1927. Generally uneven attempt to fathom the mind (and heart) of Disraeli. Some interesting insights, however.

Pearson, Hesketh. *Dizzy: The Life and Personality of Benjamin Disraeli, Earl of Beaconsfield*. New York: Harper's, 1951. Readable and entertaining; Pearson's major failure is that he is too ready to dismiss Disraeli's novels—although he usually dismisses them in a delightful manner.

Rosa, Matthew Whiting. *The Silver-Fork School: Novels of Fashion Preceding "Vanity Fair."* New York: Columbia University Press, 1936. Valuable for the reader who wishes to examine the "school" out of which Disraeli's early novels grew.

Roth, Cecil. *Benjamin Disraeli, Earl of Beaconsfield*. New York:

Philosophical Library, 1952. Best lengthy study of Disraeli's Hebrew consciousness. Roth's few conjectures are usually buttressed by convincing argument and documentation.

Speare, Morris E. *The Political Novel*. New York: Oxford University Press, 1924. One of the first critics to grapple with the problem of defining the political novel, Speare focuses principally on Disraeli; and, although the book ultimately fails in its broader attempt at definition, it offers many important insights for the student of both the novel and Disraeli. Speare also discusses the influence of Carlyle on Disraeli.

Stephen, Leslie. *Hours in a Library (Second Series)*. London: Smith, Elder, 1878. Stephen cannot take Disraeli's novels seriously, but he is generally charmed by them—as the reader is by Stephen's chapter.

Swinnerton, Frank. "Disraeli as Novelist," *Yale Review*, XVII (Jan., 1928), 283-300. Important article in which Swinnerton argues that Disraeli came to write political novels only after he had experienced little success with his romantic novels. An interesting thesis.

Traill, H. D. "The Political Novel," *The New Fiction*. New York: Hurst and Blackett, 1897. Another attempt to treat the subject of the political novel. Traill sees the genre having begun with Disraeli. Speare is more successful than Traill, but the whole question needs much work.

Williams, Raymond. *Culture and Society 1780-1950*. New York: Columbia University Press, 1958. Although Disraeli is only one of many writers treated in this splendid book, Williams' discussion of *Sybil*, in particular, is important.

Index